SHUNNED WHISTLE-BLOWER REHABILITATED

California Taxpayers Foot the Bill for One Million Dollars

RICHARD KRUPP, PH.D.

ISBN: 1478378905

ISBN 13: 9781478378907

Library of Congress Control Number: 2012914456
CreateSpace, North Charleston, SC

When you want to help people, you tell them the truth. When you want to help yourself, you tell them what they want to hear.

Thomas Sowell, *The Thomas Sowell Reader, 2011*

.

Contents

Introduction

For nearly forty years I worked in the California prison system. During that time I met a lot of criminals and politicians. As a prison counselor, I interviewed more than seven thousand inmates, spent more than five hundred hours in group therapy with another thousand inmates, and was nearly killed by one. While working in the central office, I was harassed by the prison system executive staff, became a whistle-blower, and was eventually appointed to an executive position by Governor Schwarzenegger after being "rehabilitated." The taxpayers were forced to foot the bill for the harassment to the tune of a half million dollars. The state also had about twenty-two lawyers working on the case at a cost of about a half a million dollars. I wanted only to do my job.

Most people work, obey the law, and earn what they accumulate and accomplish. Another group of people take what they want. They don't spend the time and effort to earn anything. The criminals take our possessions and our personal safety through various means, including violence. Locking up the criminals keeps them from continuing to prey on regular citizens. It also serves as a warning to other potential criminals and those not yet apprehended. Being a criminal is a choice and goes hand in hand with substance abuse, dysfunctional relationships, and a variety of other negative behaviors. All this costs the taxpayers dearly.

I spent about three years working in the California Department of Corrections (CDC) Office of Substance Abuse Programs (OSAP). There I managed the program section and for a short time was in charge of the entire office.

By the time they get to state prison, most attempts to rehabilitate criminals are a waste of time and money. The "rule of thirds" seems to apply: About one third of the people who go to prison the first time choose to make the changes necessary to stay out once they are released. Another third don't seem to mind prison and will keep coming back each time they are released. They think of prison as home. They go out on vacation, only to return after committing more crimes. The remaining third can go either way, but it is nearly impossible to figure out how to coax them in the right direction. The best "treatment" for criminality is the aging process. As people approach the age of forty, they tend to reduce or eliminate their criminal ways.

In a UCLA study (Hser, Y-I.; Hoffman, V.; Grella, C.E.; and Anglin, M.D. A 33-year follow-up of narcotics addicts. *Archives of General Psychiatry* 58(5):503-508, 2001), a group of inmates incarcerated at California Rehabilitation Center, part of the Civil Addict Program, was followed for thirty-three years. About half of the people were dead by the age of forty. Of those remaining, one-third was in prison, one-third seemed to have gone on the straight and narrow, and one-third moved around the criminal justice system.

As far as politicians are concerned, very few are looking out for the best interests of taxpayers. Many are like the shape-shifters of mythology or science fiction: they change appearance depending on who they are talking to. Maybe this is related to the likelihood they were lawyers before becoming politicians. The people in the California legislature view tax dollars as someone would lottery winnings: easy come, easy go. It is easy to spend other people's money, especially when much of the spending is disguised or hidden. Maybe politicians are just criminals who give the appearance of being good citizens: shape-shifters.

These shape-shifters in the prison system had no problem hiding the hundreds of millions they were spending on overtime, the more than a million dollars to deal with my first whistle-blowing case, then more than a billion dollars on worthless drug-treatment programs for inmates. The taxpayers are forced to pay billions more for unnecessary medical care then get further shafted by the release of thousands of inmates. The criminals may be in the state capitol. The meat puppets in the CDC secretary's office smile and nod as their strings are pulled.

My career in the California prison system started with my being a Correctional Officer at the California Institution for Men in 1972.

How did I get from this beginning to the rehabilitated whistle-blower with a governor's appointment? This book is a compilation of personal recollections and stories about people I met along the way, providing the reader with some historical background and stories that are amusing and, in some cases, tragic or disturbing.

During the time I was working in headquarters (1984–2010), I had an opportunity to work with several directors (later Secretary)[2] who ran the prison system. By far the best and brightest leaders were Director Jim Gomez and Chief Deputy Director Bob Denninger. Though Jim did not have a prison operations background, he had a keen understanding of systems and was a quick learner. For the most part, he relied on Bob as a knowledge base for prison custody and operational expertise. Together, these two men knew what they were doing and things ran as smooth as can be expected in a large prison operation.

In 1997 Cal Terhune became director, and things started going downhill fast. Terhune lacked the integrity that I saw in the prior administration. Ed Alameida took over in 2001 and continued the downward slide. He fancied himself a fiscal expert, but was unable to manage the prison system as Director. As the Director function became the Secretary job, Rod Hickman and Jeannie Woodford took over in 2004. The two of them were less than competent. They guided the department to settlements in two large lawsuits in 2006.

Hickman and Woodford brought us down even further, bringing in a Federal Receiver over inmate medical care and wiping out the California Youth Authority. These two disasters not only destroyed any cohesion in the department operations, but also cost the taxpayers billions of dollars. Jim Tilton took over in April 2006, but operated with the cement boots left over from the Hickman/Woodford days.

The last Secretary I worked with was Matt Cate, a lawyer who surrounded himself with a small contingent he worked with at the Office of the Inspector General (OIG). The tiny operation he

---

2 The director of the CDC reported to the governor's secretary of the Youth and Adult Correctional Agency (YACA) until 2005. Legislation combined the departments as the California Department of Corrections and Rehabilitation (CDCR). The CDCR reported to the secretary of the agency after that.

came from was not in any way similar to the large complex prison system he took over. Instead of relying on the wealth of knowledge available both in headquarters and the field, he surrounded himself with lawyers. He was well insulated. I believe he will be remembered as a dismantler. During his tenure the department was diminished in its ability to manage and supervise inmates. The community became a safer place for criminals.

Governor Brown signed a bill recently to bring a bullet train to California at a cost of about $68 billion or so. Though a majority of taxpayers did not want the fast train to nowhere, the politicians apparently know what is best for the mass of ordinary California citizens. The governor calls us "declinists—who want to put their head in a hole and hope reality changes." Here I thought he was talking about himself and his fellow legislators' release of masses of inmates to the community. How many prisons would the $68 billion buy?

I

CIM — The California Institution for Men — Chino

It was October 1972. I was in the middle of the nine-month probationary program for Correctional Officers at the California Institution for Men. The prison was built in 1941. When I started working there, the prison administration had just initiated a new employee training program. I spent one week on a tour of the prison and the second week shadowing the man I would be replacing when he went on to another assignment. We were supposed to work three months on each watch. I had spent my first ninety days on third watch from four in the afternoon till midnight working in the West Dorm housing unit. It was actually a cellblock, but the doors were always kept unlocked. This was a minimum-security prison where the original wall that was intended to be a perimeter wall was now being used by the inmates for handball games.

My second ninety days were supposed to be spent on second watch working from eight in the morning until four in the afternoon, but I had aggravated Sergeant Morgan and Lieutenant Peters by speaking to Superintendent Griggs about working conditions. Only three of the twelve prisons at the time had wardens; superintendents ran the others. Bertram Griggs was the superintendent at CIM at the time. He later got into some trouble with the local game warden when Griggs was discovered using a shotgun for duck hunting on prison grounds. He also had some problems when inmate Jaime Sandoval was seen in town at the local shopping mall. Evidently Sandoval had a special arrangement that allowed him to leave the institution for haircuts and other services.

One day when I was sitting on a folding chair set along the perimeter on the minimum-security part of the institution, Griggs approached me. He asked how I liked the new arrangement that called for Correctional Officers to be posted at each of the corners around the square-shaped housing perimeter after dark. Evidently there had been a few escapes recently from the minimum side and some inmates from the nearby Camp Prado. (The campers hadn't really escaped. They walked out of the camp dorm at night and walked down the street to a Chino liquor store. They brought back some liquor and got drunk.)

Each perimeter Officer had a folding chair and a handheld radio. It wasn't too bad when the sun started going down and the afternoon heat dissipated. The flies seemed to stick to you like they had glue on their feet. The smell of manure hung in the air from the nearby dairy farms after it rained. Once the sun went down, the mosquitoes would come out. I told the superintendent about the bug problem, and he said he would see what he could do to make the job a little easier.

The next day each of the officers posted on the perimeter were provided with an inoperable car or old pickup truck to sit in. It helped with the flies and mosquitoes, but when the lieutenant found out I had talked to Griggs, I got a job change that moved me right past second watch and on to first watch, working from midnight to eight in the morning.

It was a real pain getting used to the night shift—working when most normal people are sleeping. One morning after getting off the night shift working in Redwood Hall for the first time, I heard a knock at my front door. I was living in an apartment in Chino off Philadelphia Street. I opened the door and saw Officer Felix, who I recognized from work. He was dressed in his uniform and looked nervous. He said, "We need you to come with us." I could see only Felix through the peephole.

"Who is *we*, and why should I come with you?"

Another guy came out from behind the bushes, dressed in a blue flowered shirt and beige pants. He announced, "I am Sergeant Hernandez. I'm an investigator, and you need to come with us *voluntarily* or I will have to *arrest* you."

I understood what he was saying, but had no idea what I had done that would create this predicament. With no verbal response, I got into the backseat of the cage car, and they closed the door. I noticed the doors didn't have inside handles, and there was no way for me to get out unless someone opened the door from the outside.

"What is this about?"

For the life of me I could not figure out why I was being treated like an inmate. I had been working at the prison for only a couple of months. I knew they didn't like the way I wore my hair, and inmates had complained about my squeaky boots waking them up when I walked down the hallways taking count at night, but this was a little extreme. As we approached the gatehouse, I noticed there were extra officers, and two of them looked at me in the backseat. They looked at me the way you look at someone you caught stealing your car or beating your dog.

"What happened? Did someone escape?" I asked.

As soon as the words left my lips, Felix and Hernandez snapped their necks to the side and looked at each other then back at me. I must have said some magic words, but not the kind that open doors for you or win the prize.

We drove to the administration building and parked by the brass doors leading to the superintendent's office. Felix opened the rear door and let me out. I was escorted into the office and told to sit in the folding chair. Managers I had seen before, but didn't know, surrounded me. The lieutenant was the only familiar face. Everybody looked at me with disgust. The inquisition started. First they asked innocuous questions. How long have you worked here?

"Just a few months."

You have a college degree; why would you want to work here?

"I thought I might help some of the inmates change their ways."

The questions came from all directions. I began to block out the looks and side conversations. My stomach began to feel like I wanted to vomit, but I was still under control. The barrage paused for a moment. I think they realized I was getting focused and not breaking down.

The daggers came out again. "Do you know an inmate named Ross?"

"No, I don't."

"Well, he lives in Redwood Hall. That's where you work. Don't you know the inmates in your dorm?"

I still didn't know why I was here, but I did know that they didn't do their homework. "I just started working in Redwood Hall last night. I haven't had a chance to get to know all of the inmates there. They were all asleep during my midnight shift." I could tell by the reaction in the room that they were not aware I had worked in Redwood Hall only one night.

"Inmate Ross escaped, and we think you helped get him out of the prison." There it was, out on the table. I paused for a moment.

"I drove out of the prison this morning when my shift was over. My car and trunk were checked by the gate officer when I left. If I helped someone escape, how could I get them out of here?"

They appeared stumped. Hernandez stood up and said, "We think you got him past the gate somehow and drove him down the street then let him out."

I couldn't believe what I was hearing. "That's absurd. How could I get him through the gate without being seen? Why would I help someone escape anyway?" I was back in focus.

"We think you may have helped him because you are a college graduate and may be trying to help the inmates."

I couldn't believe this. What kind of investigators do we have working here? "First of all, I did not help anyone escape. Your theory about the escape is ridiculous." I think once the theories and innuendos were spoken, they realized none of it made any sense.

There were some side conversations, then the lieutenant said, "I think we are done here. The officer will drive you back home."

"Wait a minute. You wake me up, force me to come down here to an inquisition, accuse me of some absurd plot, then tell me to go home and forget about it?"

"We will get back to you soon." I couldn't believe it. These managers seemed like a bunch of buffoons. How could people like this run a prison?

I did think I could help inmates out by talking to them and helping them see the errors of their criminal ways. I wanted to apply some of the theories I had studied while at California State University in Northridge. Before coming to work for the CDC, I had completed my bachelor's degree with a major in sociology. I worked forty hours a week and took five to six classes a semester to finish in two years after completing an associate's degree at a community college.

Over the course of the next couple of weeks, I would get suspicious looks from some of the other officers, but no one really talked about the incident. I went to talk to Captain Kelly two weeks after the inquisition. He said they determined I had nothing to do with the escape of inmate Ross. I asked if he would put something in my personnel file to show that I was subjected to a rather strange detention and investigation. The captain indicated there would be no mention of it in my file—just like it never happened.

I wrote letters to the union and to the deputy director in Sacramento. Everybody seemed to think my best course of action was to forget about the incident. It didn't feel right, but I dropped it and moved on. This left me with an uneasy feeling. I wanted everyone to know that I had been treated unjustly. I didn't want the suspicious stares anymore. I wanted to be able to talk about the incident freely. I didn't want to feel that I had anything to hide. It was an uncomfortable feeling that I would later learn to embrace.

The California correctional officers were starting to organize at this time. There were competing groups that included the California State Employees Association (CSEA), the Teamsters, and the upstart California Correctional Officers Association that would later become the California Correctional Peace Officers Association (CCPOA). You could join all three of the groups and pay two to six dollars in dues each month. I asked for assistance with my inquisition problem, but none of the union people wanted to get involved. At that time I was earning $561 per month. We were allowed to have only the department uniform patch on one sleeve, and the only badge was on our hat. Some officers still wore the old khaki uniforms instead of the green pants worn today.

CIM in the News

CIM saw several headline-grabbing incidents over the years. The first that I can recall happened during my time as a correctional officer.

We worked a straight eight-hour shift. Everyone arrived fifteen minutes early for the watch meeting to find out if there were any things going on that we needed to know. At that time we didn't get paid for the fifteen minutes. We also talked about special events coming up like when Cheech and Chong were planning a visit to entertain the inmates. We did find time to go to the personnel kitchen, or PK, if we worked a patrol position, like I had. I had just finished my rounds looking for security problems and sat down in the PK for a cheeseburger and fries. At the table next to me was Jesse Sanchez. Jesse was one of those officers who looked sharp. His uniform was always pressed and all of his equipment in the right place. He was very professional, as opposed to some of the other correctional officers on first watch.

During my first one hundred days there had been a couple of serious incidents, including an inmate getting murdered in the academic education area between classes. Evidently this involved some kind of gang dispute. But on October 6, 1972, something terrible happened. A group known as the Venceremos concocted a scheme that started with a fake court appearance. The institution received a document indicating inmate Ronald Beatty was needed for a court hearing, and transport arrangements were made. The inmate was placed in the back of the vehicle driven by an unarmed correctional officer and another unarmed officer in the passenger seat. They drove outside the institution down a side road and were ambushed.

Officers Jesse Sanchez and George Fitzgerald were stopped by members of the Venceremos and shot. Jesse died that day, but George survived. Six custody staff had been killed by inmates the year before and two the year before that.

Correctional Officer Jesse Sanchez

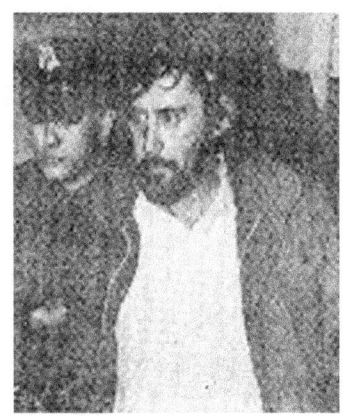

Ronald Beatty

According to the Palo Alto History Project[2],

Ronald Beaty, a Venceremos recruit, was serving time at CIM for armed robbery and kidnapping. Beaty apparently had romantic ties to Jean Hobson—the former Venceremos candidate for Palo Alto City council.

According to police and Beaty, who would become the prosecution's star witness, the state car was forced off a remote highway road near Chino. Four Venceremos members jumped out of two vehicles to set Beaty free. As they prepared to flee the scene, 23-year-old Venceremos member Robert Seabok shot both officers at point blank range, killing 24-year-old Jesus Sanchez and wounding his partner George Fitzgerald. Venceremos members Hobson, Seabok, Andrea Holman Burt and Benton Burt were named as the other ambushers.

---

2 Palo Alto History Project.com

Hobson and Beaty, possessing a trunk-load of weapons, were arrested two months later on the Bay Bridge by San Francisco police without incident. Beaty named the four members who helped him escape. He identified Robert Seabok as the gunman, and described how other members of Venceremos helped hide him in a rural San Mateo County mountain cabin for close to a month. Beaty pleaded guilty for his involvement in Sanchez's death and received a life sentence. All four Venceremos members would eventually be found guilty in subsequent trials. Jean Hobson, 19-year-old Andrea Holman Burt, and 31-year-old Douglas Burt were all found guilty of second-degree murder in 1973 and 1974, and Seabok got life imprisonment and a first-degree murder conviction.

Following their legal difficulties related to the incident at Chino, Venceremos began to come apart at the seams. Arguments erupted between various factions in the organization and members began to pull out and join other groups. By September of 1973, Venceremos had officially disbanded. Many ex-Venceremos members went on to other organizations, including the SLA (Symbionese Liberation Army) group that assassinated Oakland superintendent Dr. Marcus Foster at a school board meeting in November 1973 and then kidnapped newspaper heiress Patricia Hearst in February of 1974.

RONALD WAYNE BEATY   JEAN S. HOBSON

CIM Kevin Cooper

The second major incident at CIM occurred when I worked the reception center as a correctional counselor[3]. In June 1983 a man convicted of burglary under the name David Troutman was sent to the minimum facility for processing because the reception center was too full.

We learned later that his real name was Kevin Cooper, and he was wanted in Pennsylvania for burglary, kidnapping, and rape. In June he escaped by cutting a hole through the perimeter fence. He was later convicted of murdering Franklin Ryen, his wife, their ten-year old daughter, and eleven-year-old neighbor . The Ryens' eight-year-old son barely survived the gruesome attack that reads like something from a horror movie.

There have been stories of Cooper's innocence that point the blame at three mysterious men who were the real culprits. I actually was drawn into the legend, having heard about the mysterious three men from an inmate I interviewed a short time after the murders. He told me about the three men bragging about the crime when he was in jail with them. Years later I testified about

---

3 Typical duties included an interview with inmates newly committed to prison after transfer from county jail. The inmates were classified for transfer to another prison for more permanent housing.

the conversation at a federal court hearing. As often happens, memories become less acute over the years. I could not accurately recall to whom I had passed the information on.

The endless appeals have dragged the death sentence on and created a veritable fan club for Cooper. Lost in all the misguided support for the convicted murderer are the families forever haunted by the nightmare.

CIM Later Years

Years later, in January 2005, death would visit another correctional officer at CIM. Inmate Jon Blaylock arrived at CIM on June 23, 2004. Less than four months after he was released from prison the last time, Blaylock was stopped by a police officer for riding a bicycle without a headlight. Blaylock got into a shoot-out with the officer. Though he fired four shots at the officer, no one was injured.

Blaylock was housed at the institution's reception center for more than six months, pending permanent placement at another institution. He had a history of violent behavior toward correctional employees and other inmates, had served prior prison terms for attempted burglary and robbery, and was now in prison with a seventy-five-year sentence for the attempted murder of a police officer. During prior prison stints, Blaylock spent a lot of time in administrative segregation because of violent behavior, but this time he was considered an influential inmate, so he was often released from his cell to confer with other inmates and help ease racial tensions on the tier. (There had been a riot between black and Hispanic inmates the month before.)

CIM had delayed issuing the 362 stab-proof vests it received in September 2004 to correctional officers while updating policies on vest distribution. There were not yet enough vests for all those designated to receive them, and the prison didn't want to deal with complaints of unfairness, so they stored the vests they had in the warehouse. Evidently the prison had received about half the number of vests they needed for the officers. One option would have been to get together with the union and prioritize distributing vests they did have, pending delivery of the remainder of the order.

This sort of convoluted thought process was typical for the CDC. Management had been so whipsawed between various court orders and union actions that apparent commonsense decisions were hard to come by. It reminded me of the opposite position recommended by Yogi Berra: "When you get to a fork in the road, take it." For the CDC, it had become, "When you get to a fork in the road, wait and take no action." Rarely does indecision work out well: no decision *is* a decision. A stab-proof protective vest personally fitted for and assigned to Officer Gonzalez was in the warehouse when the stabbing occurred.

On Monday, January 10, 2005, Sycamore Hall housed 213 inmates with four correctional officers working second watch, responsible for inmate supervision and escort. Officer Manual Gonzalez, forty-three-year-old father of six and sixteen-year CDC veteran, released thirty-five-year-old Blaylock from his cell. The earliest Blaylock was eligible for parole was January 23, 2071. Less than two weeks earlier, the first-tier grill gate was opened against modified program procedures, and, as a result, a white inmate stabbed a black inmate. On the morning of January 10, one of Officer Gonzalez's coworkers had warned him that letting Blaylock out of his cell onto the tier through the grill gate and entering the tier alone to talk to the inmate was dangerous and could result in a stabbing. Usually when inmates were out of their cells on the tiers, the officers would be on the other side of the grill gates. The warning was prescient.

The routine at the reception center, which included transferring five hundred to seven hundred inmates in and an equal amount out every week, dulled your sense of caution. There was constant loud talking, door clanging, and an occasional thunderous sound you could hear when a large number of correctional officers responded to a disturbance. It was a welcome sound if you were one of a handful of officers working a cell block where a group of inmates were engaged in a stabbing or fight. Even though you are surrounded by violent caged murderers and assorted other criminals, you grow comfortable with the tension. You don't even feel the pressure that surrounds you until you stop working in a prison.

According to an investigation conducted by the OIG[4],

Gonzalez directed another officer to unlock Blaylock's cell so he could have access to the tier and try to calm racial tensions. The officer refused, asking Gonzalez how they would explain it "if he stabs somebody." Gonzalez said no one would get stabbed and opened the cell himself. He subsequently returned Blaylock to his cell while other officers released White and Hispanic inmates for medical appointments. After the White and Black inmates left, other officers working in the unit released eight Black inmates from their cells for medical appointments and had those eight inmates wait in the guard space. At that point Gonzalez asked that Blaylock again be released from his cell and onto the tier. Shortly thereafter, two Hispanic permanent work crew inmates arrived unsupervised to make plumbing repairs at Sycamore Hall in a cell occupied by two Black inmates. Even though modified program restrictions were still in effect, and even though the front door of the housing unit was open, Gonzalez opened the grill gate to allow one of the two Hispanic permanent work crew inmates to enter the tier.

The two Black inmates who were occupying the cell needing the plumbing repair should have been moved to a secure area while the repairs were made, instead officers told them to come out of the cell and stand on the tier against the wall. An officer then opened the front door of the housing unit to release the eight Black inmates to medical appointments. At that moment, and while the door was open, a White inmate

---

4 Special Review into the Death of Correctional Officer Manual A. Gonzalez Jr. on January 10, 2005 at the California Institution for Men

returned from a medical appointment unannounced and walked up the corridor toward the entrance to Sycamore Hall. One officer then left the guard space to control the White inmate, leaving three officers in the guard space including Gonzalez, to watch eight Black inmates, the Hispanic plumber, the two Black inmates who had been released from their cell because of the plumbing repair, and Blaylock. Meanwhile, Blaylock and the two Black inmates who had been released for the plumbing repair began roaming up and down the stairs to all three tiers of the living unit. At that point one of the three officers was distracted by a telephone call and, simultaneously, Blaylock called to Gonzalez, asking him to enter the tier. In response Gonzalez again opened the grill gate, with the front door to the housing unit still open, and went onto the tier alone to speak to Blaylock. At about 10:57 that morning, immediately after Officer Gonzalez entered the tier he was stabbed by Blaylock.

After being stabbed multiple times in the chest, Officer Gonzalez made his way to the guard space and then collapsed. Witnesses described the first-tier guard space as "pandemonium." As many as twenty-five correctional officers crowded into the guard space where eight inmates were on the floor and the air was filled with pepper spray. The downed officer was carried to the medical clinic by his fellow officers. Two physicians were present when the wounded man was brought into the clinic. Typically the prison medical staff performed cursory exams of inmates new to prison or those with complaints that ranged from the serious to the veiled attempts to get pills for recreational use. On occasion there would be the need to patch up inmates after a fistfight or stabbing with makeshift weapons, but rarely would a staff member be in need of medical treatment. This time the need for doctors trained in emergency medical care was great, but the response was lacking.

The medical aid provided to Officer Gonzalez that day at CIM could be described as bumbling. There was a lack of proper equipment, and when the equipment was there, medical staff members were not familiar with its use. Procedures were done incorrectly or not at all. No one was prepared for an incident of this magnitude. By 11:10 a.m. a medic engine from the local community fire department 2.5 miles away arrived and initiated treatment. The ambulance left the institution at 11:20 a.m., arriving at the Chino Valley Medical Center ten minutes later. At 11:52 a.m., Officer Manual Gonzalez was pronounced dead.

A comprehensive search of Sycamore Hall after the murder of Officer Gonzalez uncovered thirty-five weapons that had been secreted in the inmate cells. It is difficult to determine whether a stab-proof vest would have protected Officer Gonzalez. The assailant might have gone after other vital areas of the body. The protective vests were taken from the warehouse and distributed to the CIM correctional officers a few days later.

There was speculation that Blaylock, with the assistance of the two inmates with the plumbing problem, carried out the attack on Officer Gonzalez in retaliation for the stabbing of a black inmate two weeks earlier. The theory was that the stabbing was enabled because the correctional officers on duty allowed access to the tier.

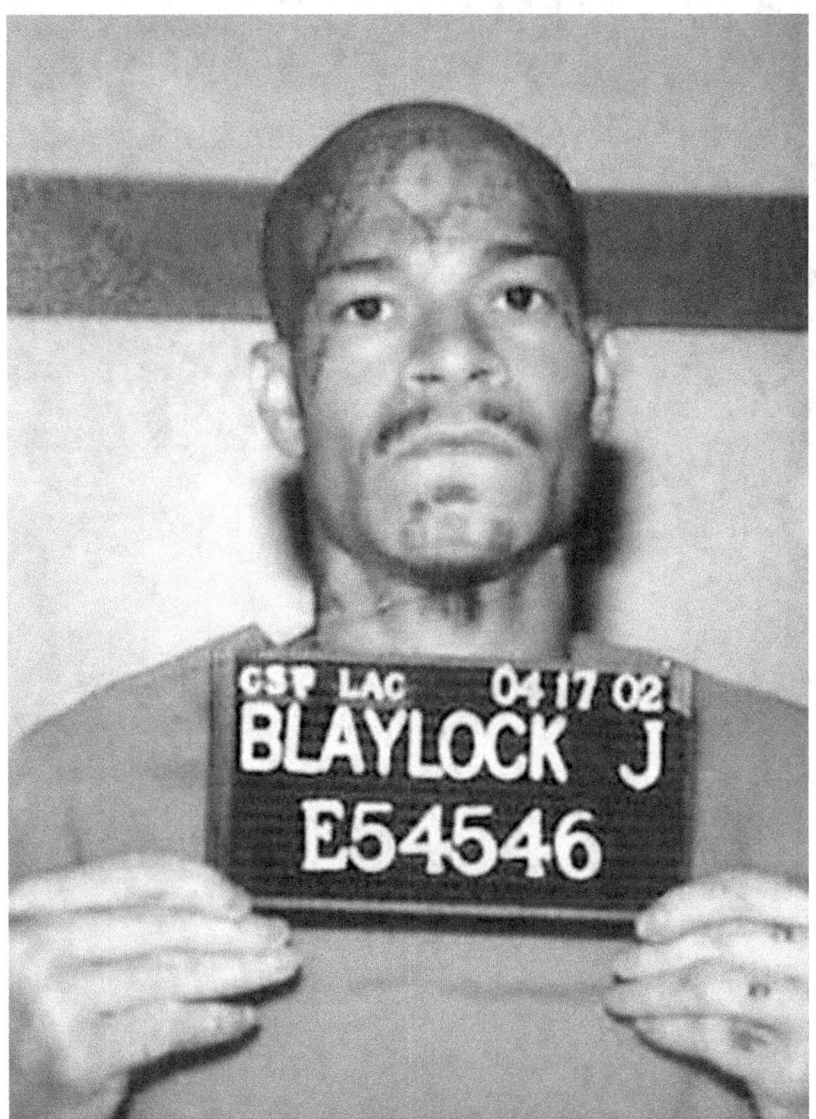

California Department of Corrections

In Memoriam

Manuel A. Gonzalez Jr.

Born
September 15, 1961

Entered into Rest
January 10, 2005

Family Acknowledgements

The Gonzalez family wishes to thank everyone for their thoughts, love, and prayers during this tragic time.

2

CRC — The California Rehabilitation Center — Norco

By October 1973 I had finished probation at CIM and put in for a transfer to the CRC in Norco, just a few miles away. This was a rather odd place that at one time had been a resort hotel for Hollywood stars, a naval hospital, and was now a prison for drug addicts. The men here were not considered inmates. They were drug addicts who had been committed for treatment under the Welfare and Institutions Civil Code. It was run by the department of corrections and staffed with correctional staff, but uniforms for officers were optional. The inmates were called residents. They wore regular inmate blue jeans with white T-shirts or blue chambray, while you could see correctional officers in yellow seersucker pants and platform shoes. There were swimming pools inside and outside the main buildings that were used by residents and staff members.

I worked in the service unit or hotel section of the institution. There was also a section up at the top of the hill that has occasionally housed female addicts or inmates. During this time the female section was vacant. The CDC was downsizing, since the prison population was decreasing. Some prisons were scheduled to close. My dorm was called Dorm Eight, or the Veterans' Dorm. Each dorm of residents had a theme. In Dorm Eight all of the residents had been in a branch of the military service. Each dorm operated under certain program requirements that would determine if there were group therapy sessions and/or work assignments. There was a correctional counselor assigned to each dorm to run the large group sessions involving about sixty residents and small group sessions of six to ten residents each. These were typically called attack groups.

My assignment was third watch, so I mainly watched the residents after group or work activities. I took count often, handed out aspirins, and talked a lot. I was only vaguely aware at the time there was a research project under way that was looking at each dorm to determine which program had the best outcomes—which residents stayed out of CRC after being released to outpatient status, as they called it. Some residents would start using drugs when they got out then turn themselves in at the gate to get back in. We called them gate-turn-ins. Unfortunately, it seems that the control group, which had regular work assignments and no group therapy, had the best outcomes.

Once again I found myself on first watch. This time I had aggravated Sergeant Bates to no end by refusing to cut my hair short. It wasn't really that long, but Bates wanted me to have my hair cut short. I had run into that problem at CIM before, but discovered there wasn't any sort of departmental regulation requiring short hair. Sergeant Bates solved the problem by assigning me to a tower. While on tower duty, I was required to watch the fence line and call in on the radio every half hour. This mind-numbing experience drove me to take a test to work in the California Youth Authority. I took the youth counselor test and scored high enough to be in the top rank on the list.

3

California Youth Authority
YTS – Youth Training School – Ontario

In October 1973 I went to work at the Youth Training School as a youth counselor. The young men who stayed here were called wards, ranging in age from about sixteen to twenty-five. Each counselor performed correctional officer custody functions like counts and searches and also performed casework and group therapy. The caseloads were small—six to ten wards—and the paperwork was minimal. Some of the wards I worked with went on to become active members of the Mexican Mafia, including Daniel Barela and Daniel and Senon Grajeda. This was the most violent place I ever worked. While I was there, we had an escape from the lockup housing unit known as O&R Company. Wards got out of their cells and escaped into the nearby cornfield. On the way out, they beat one of our staff members in the head with a fire extinguisher, causing major injuries.

Wards assaulted me at least six times during my brief eight months at YTS. In January 1974 I escorted a group of wards from W&X Company to the yard to play basketball. As it started to get dark, I ordered the group to return to the housing unit. On the way back, some of the wards decided to take a detour and broke into the canteen. This was basically the convenience store where the wards could purchase snacks and other small items during the day with funds that were placed in their trust accounts by family members. I entered the door to the canteen and saw a couple of the wards stuffing food items into their shirts.

I identified one of the Wards as John Carter, from W&X Company. When I got back to the control room, I wrote up a report of the incident. As it turned out, Carter was scheduled to be released on parole the following week and as a result of the canteen incident, was going to have to stay at YTS a while longer. In addition, he was to remain locked in his cell for a couple of weeks. This of course did not make him very happy. On January 14, 1974, John Carter got his revenge.

Each of the housing units had a control center with doors you could close to seal off the center from the cell units on either side. Typically we left the doors to the control room open. On this day, someone pulled the lever in the control center and let Carter out of his cell. I was going through the file cabinet in the center of the control room. I saw someone approaching me so I turned to my right. In a flash Cater swung his right fist and hit me on the side of the face. The force of his punch turned me to the left. I stumbled, and my mouth connected with the sink on the side of the control room. Carter pulled me back from the sink, and I fell to the floor, staring up at the ceiling.

I looked up at him and could see him staring into my eyes with a look that scared me. I could see, but couldn't move. Carter had grabbed a baseball bat from behind the control room door and had raised it like a batter ready to swing at a fastball—only in this case, the baseball was my head. I could see his eyes widen as he began his swing, but I couldn't move. Then out of nowhere came Jesse Edwards, one of the youth counselors I worked with. Jesse wrapped his arms around Carter and pulled him away mid-swing. Jesse was a man with a big smile and a personality that always made you feel at ease. One minute, I was certain that I was going to either be dead or have my head rearranged; the next, an angel rescued me.

After Jesse whisked Carter away, I pulled myself up off the floor, feeling like a car had hit me. My supervisor told me I didn't look too good and should go to the institution hospital for an exam. I remember walking out of the housing unit and across the field, but then I couldn't remember where I was going. I stopped and stood still. One of the wards on my caseload, Harold Johnson, approached me. "Mr. Krupp, you don't look so good. Where are you going?" I don't remember what I said, but he escorted me to the institution hospital. The doctor looked at my bloody eye and asked if I knew my name or where I was. I told him I knew the answer to both questions, but just couldn't tell him. He told me to wait there until I could answer the questions.

The amnesia soon faded, but the chipped teeth have remained—something to remember John Carter by. Because of the injury, the institution let me go home two hours early, but I had to be back at work the next day.

My days at YTS were peppered with several strange events. A hanging was the other major incident I played a role in. I was working the afternoon shift from two until ten at night in February 1974. One of my coworkers, O'Conner, was having some trouble with one of the wards all day. Our supervisor, Mr. David, suggested an in-cell confrontation. Evidently, when there were problems between staff and wards, the recommended solution was for the staff member to go to the ward's cell and lock himself in with the guy. He would then fight with the ward until they worked things out.

O'Conner went down to the cell, and we pulled the lever in the control room, locking the door. You could hear scuffling all the way down the hallway. O'Conner was twenty-eight years old and about six feet tall with a muscular build, weighing in at about 225 pounds. The ward, Martinez, was all of about five and a half feet tall, 145 pounds, and nineteen years old. After a few minutes, the scuffling stopped. I walked down the hall to check in on the fight and see how they were doing. When I peeked through the small window in the cell door I saw O'Conner up against the wall with Martinez applying a headlock that seemed to be pretty effective. O'Conner signaled that he had had enough. I went back to the control room and racked[5] the cell door open.

---

5 Racking a door open involved pulling a lever in the control room

O'Conner came out of the cell, his face red and his clothes disheveled. He was angry and embarrassed. Martinez stayed in his cell. Word got around quickly and eventually got back to our supervisor, Mr. David.

Since I had been assaulted by wards a couple of times, Mr. David suggested I pick out one of the troublesome wards on the unit and take him into one of the holding cells and beat him up, to help gain some respect among the wards. I found the idea foolish and declined the suggestion. It then became more than a suggestion. Mr. David said it was an order. This was a decision point that, like others in the future, would become etched in my memory. I can remember the expression on Mr. David's face and somehow knew this meant there would be consequences if I picked the wrong response. Again I refused. I was notified of my shift change by a note on the sign-in sheet. Starting the next day, I would be working from ten at night until six in the morning, the new "night man."

My second week as the night man, I was walking down the tier at midnight, making my rounds and taking count. It was a tedious job. Every half hour I would walk past each cell and look inside to see if the ward assigned to that cell was there. At each end of the hallways, there was a count slip taped to the wall. I had to sign the slip and indicate the count time and the number of wards I counted. After passing one of the cells for the fourth or fifth time, I noticed that one of the wards was standing by the back of the cell looking out the window. He had been in this position for several counts. I asked him what he was doing, but he didn't say anything; he didn't even move. It looked suspicious to me, so I called for the counselor from the next housing unit to come over and cover me while I went into the cell to find out what was going on. When I got closer, I realized he wasn't standing in the back looking out the window—he was hanging from the window. He had attached his belt to the window bar, tightened it around his neck, and bent his knees. This guy had hanged himself.

We cut him down from the window and loosened the belt, but it was too late. His face was a purplish gray, and his tongue was hanging out. He was dead. The only other time I had been that close to a corpse was when I worked at CIM the year before in the hospital. My job then included taking fingerprints on the old inmates who had died in the middle of the night. I had seen that cold gray look before, which made me feel like my stomach was in knots, and I could feel my heart beating. Working at YTS was growing more and more like a bad dream. I had been there only five months, but I had been attacked six times, almost killed, and seen stabbings, beat-downs, and now a hanging. What a nightmare.

The next week I was working the two-to-ten shift on a hot summer afternoon. Most of the other staff had taken groups of wards out to the yard to play basketball and just hang out. My supervisor, Mr. David, and I were left watching over about twenty-five wards sitting in the dayroom playing cards and watching TV. We were in the control room talking about sports and women. Nothing indicated there was any tension in the air. Then I heard a couple of wards talking loudly in the rear corner of the dayroom. When I looked up, I saw two red-faced guys standing up with their bare chests inflated and looks of rage in their eyes.

Somehow the group of twenty-five wards had grown to at least fifty. I don't know when they came into the dayroom, but they were forming two distinct groups. David and I looked at each other and knew what was going to happen next. David opened the window vent and started to shout, "Break it up." Before the words left his lips, the two groups engaged. I could see arms and fists flying and blood started oozing through the white T-shirts. People were getting stabbed, chairs were flying, and forty-five-pound weights were being tossed around; it was loud and smelled bad. There was a tension that engulfed the dayroom and crept into the control room and up my back. Sensory overload gave way to an instinctual feeling to "do something."

David and I looked at each other a split second. He said to me, "Open the door. Let's get out there and break it up." One of us would have to unlock the grill door in order for anyone to get in or out of the dayroom at our end. Wards were still entering the dayroom from the yard, through the back. After taking a quick look at the more than fifty wards stabbing, hitting, and kicking each other, I decided not to enter the fray. "The two of us are *not* going out there," I said. David instructed me to open the door and let him go, if I didn't want to get out there. Again I refused. I told him we were going to call for the assistance of the security squad and observe. I didn't know if this was the right decision, but I didn't think the two of us had a chance fighting the fifty people, some of them armed.

Being an indirect participant in a riot was quiet an experience. It seemed like my vision and hearing expanded. I could see and hear things all around me, but found it difficult to do anything quickly. Time and space were bigger, but I was moving in slow motion.

David paused for a moment, then agreed that we should call for help and observe. Out of nowhere we saw three wards pounding on the grill door. From the looks on their faces, I could tell they were scared and did not want to be caught up in the battle. David pulled the lever to open the grill door. As it opened, the wards squeezed in before it opened all the way. I pulled the lever to close it. After seconds that seemed to move in slow motion, the two groups moved to separate corners. You could see blood-soaked white T-shirts, scratched and bruised faces, people out of breath, and you could hear some groans and the thuds and clangs of weapons dropping to the floor.

The wards must have heard the security squad rumbling up the ramp outside. The squad seemed to enter the dayroom just as everything was over. All the wards were out of energy. The security squad sent some of the wards to the hospital for medical treatment, cuffed some, and escorted others to the holding cells in the back of the control room until the cells were filled, then took the remaining wards to the lockup unit at O& R. A few were sent to their rooms.

YTS was always a problem institution, with wards assaulting other wards and staff members. Many years later, a staff member would die. According to the California Court of Appeals, Case C036202:

The problems at YTS grew to a head on August 9, 1996. 42-year-old Ineasie Baker was walking down the hallway on C Company talking to someone following the completion of her shift at 1:00 that afternoon. A co-worker later recalled, "I heard Ms. Baker, she was going off on a ward and then just went bloop, she stopped talking." James Ferris, about 25 years old, was in YTS for the murder of a woman in 1989 who had taken him into her house. The convicted murderer was worried about being transferred to an adult prison. He decided to kill Baker and take her keys in order to escape. Ferris proceeded to beat stab and strangle Ms. Baker. Her body was stuffed into a trash can, hauled past security and emptied into a Dumpster. Ms. Baker's body was found two days later in a local landfill. In September, 2001, the piece of human waste known as James Ferris was convicted of murder and sentenced to state prison.

4

CIM — Correctional Counselor

In June 1974, two supervising counselors from CIM came to see me while I was on the job at YTS. They came on a day I had agreed to work a double shift on overtime, so I was there in the afternoon. Within each housing unit, we would make our own arrangements for sick leave and overtime. Someone would say they wanted to call in sick the next day to do something at home, and someone else would agree to work in his place and get paid time-and-a-half to boot. Not bad. The supervisors didn't have to worry about last-minute arrangements for shift coverage. Ted Fahey and Lon Cherrington were at YTS to ask me if I wanted to work at CIM on a promotion from youth counselor to "Correctional Counselor I."

I guess I had scored pretty high on the promotional exam. By July I was working at the new CIM-East Diagnostic and Treatment Center. The facility used to be part of the CYA. It was called the Older Boys Reception Center (OBRC) a few years back, then was closed around 1975. Just before it was closed, the facility had a fence erected in the middle and had male CYA wards on one side and female prison inmates on the other. The handpicked team of counselors and psychologists for CIM-East were going to be interviewing inmates who were sent to us for ninety days of testing and risk analysis. After the ninety days were over, or sometimes sooner, the inmate would be sent back to the judge for sentencing. Most of these inmates were placed on probation, with only about 20 percent headed to prison for their sentence. (This is where Roman Polanski came for testing. He stayed for forty-two days and then went back for sentencing. For some reason the judge let him out of jail pending the sentencing hearing. Polanski left the country before he was sentenced and has never returned.)

It was during this time I became involved in "attack therapy." Inmates undergoing diagnostic testing and observation were assigned a counselor and psychologist for interviews and recommendations to the court for sentencing. It became a powerful tool. A man's future could depend on how the counselor or psychologist described him in our reports. In addition to writing these evaluations, I volunteered to lead an attack therapy group. We accepted only inmates who volunteered. No reports were written regarding their participation, since we wanted only people who were serious about discussing their problems. We didn't want anyone there just to get a "good-guy" report to show the judge. An inmate who was staying at the facility on a permanent basis, Al Martinez, volunteered to run the group for me.

Al was an "A" number. All California prison inmates get a number when they go to prison. The prison numbers started with a letter (San Quentin used an all-numeric number when they first opened). We were issuing "C" numbers in 1974. Al had done a lot of time, mostly for drugs, burglaries, and robberies. He was tall, thin, and had long hair—similar to my appearance, at the time. The group met Monday through Friday each week for one hour, and three hours one evening a week; most of the time we had between five and ten other inmate participants.

At about ten each morning the inmates would show up and wait in the dayroom. Al and I would go over any concerns we had about the group dynamics and problems surrounding inmates whom Al had recruited for the group. Dave Smith came to the group for the first time on this day. We all sat in a circle of chairs in the dayroom, and everyone would introduce himself to start out. Twenty-five-year-old Rod Serrano was a short, gruff, young man who carried himself and spoke like an old gangster. He had been in the system for a few years on a murder case or, as the inmates said, "murder beef." Rod was a regular participant and helped run things. Danny Calise was a forty-something big Italian gangster-looking man in for extortion and various other violent cases.

Dave was asked to move his chair to the center of the circle and take "the hot seat." A big man with blonde hair and pink face, he looked as if he was not sure he really wanted to be there. He remained tough and moved to the center, telling his story about how he ended up in prison. "I'm here because I couldn't find a job." Dave spat out the words, then waited for a reaction. Al was first. "Hey, Dave, I don't know where you come from, but where I come from they don't send people to prison for not having a job."

Dave was beginning to turn a pinkish shade of red. He wasn't sure how to react to an inmate confronting him in front of me and other inmates. Al said, "Don't look at Mr. Krupp, Dave; he isn't going to tell anyone what you say. Nothing that is said in this room leaves this room." That was the deal I made when I put the group together. I wouldn't pass on anything that was revealed in the group.

"OK. I couldn't find a good job, so I sold some drugs." Dave was pleased with his response. Rod said, "What do you mean by *good* Job? Does that mean you had a job, but you didn't think it was *good?*"

"Yeah," Dave said. "I couldn't get anything other than working at McDonald's for minimum wage."

Rod shot back, "So how much are you making here, Dave?" Dave was at a loss for words. Al summarized: "So let's see, Dave—you had a job in the free world working for minimum wage, and you traded it in for a seat here in prison making an ass out of yourself in front of all these inmates?" No response from Dave.

Danny interjected. "Hey, Dave, how were you living if you only were pulling in minimum wage?"

Dave was a little deflated. "Well, I was staying with my girlfriend, and she had a good job."

Danny went for the throat. "So you were ashamed that you were stuck in a fast-food joint making pennies while your woman

29

was carrying you? Now I understand why you traded that in for this." The group chuckled.

Al started up another path. "What were you selling, Dave?"

"I sold some crack and some speed and some heroin."

Al spotted an opening. "People don't just start selling all that stuff one day, Dave. Sounds like you have some history here."

Dave had apparently given up trying to make himself out to be a poor soul, out of work, who committed a crime just to survive. "Well, I guess I did some time before—maybe a nickel [5 years] for dope."

Al looked smug. "Now we got you figured out, Dave. You like to do drugs, sell them to support your habit, and live off women. When you started feeling embarrassed about being a low-life worthless criminal, you came back to your comfort zone. No one expects anything from you here. No responsibilities, no bills to pay, someone tells you when to get up when to go to sleep." In less than an hour Al, Rod, and Danny, three men who were evidently wiser than any psychologist I ever met, had cut to the core of David Smith and opened him up. Dave was stunned. Al now took on a fatherly tone. "Dave, you probably feel like shit right now, but that's good. You have started the process that could help you become someone different. The first step is to look at yourself for what you are, and the picture ain't good. Keep coming to the group. All of us are just as fucked-up as you are. The only difference is we figured it out before you did." Dave looked relieved.

Al and I would have a wrap-up meeting in my office after the group meeting. Some of the guys would follow up on Dave in the evening. We wanted to make sure he made it back to the group the next day. Al wanted to talk to Dave about his "game." He wanted to know if Dave was still going with the "poor guy without a job" story, or was he going to tell his counselor and psychologist the real story when he talked to them next week?

Dave Smith went on to become one of the group leaders. I'm not sure how effective the meetings were as far as changing the inmates' behavior when they got out, but I learned a great deal from Al, Dave, Rod, Danny, and the others. They taught me to look beyond the answers to questions that are offered only to get you to stop asking questions—that "excuses only satisfy those who make them." I began to question some of the theories about criminals I had studied in college.

In July 1977 things began to change. The CIM Diagnostic and Treatment Center fell victim to Senate Bill 77. Prison was for punishment, they said. No more indeterminate sentencing. The parole board would see its role diminish, with most prison and parole terms now being set by the judge at the time of sentencing. Associate Superintendent Chuck Villalobos met with me and said I would be transferred to the CIM Reception Center Central (RCC). There would be no more diagnostic center. I was a little disturbed. For the most part, I thought we were doing some good things with the evaluations and the attack groups. I saw things from the side of the process that were hopeful. The inmates talked about how they were going to change and stay out of trouble. The move to RCC would be an eye-opener. It was certainly a bifurcation point, a fork in the road that would change my thoughts and perceptions of people forever.

Working at RCC I had a standard caseload of about fifteen inmates each week. I was a counselor in name only. The job consisted of reading the inmate's file, having one face-to-face interview, then writing a report with a recommendation for transfer to the prison where the inmate would start serving his sentence. The work was not very difficult. I started working four ten-hour days, with Friday off each week. That still wasn't enough to keep me busy, so I went back to graduate school at Claremont. They had a PhD program in criminal justice. Professor Jerry Jordan interviewed me and thought I would be a good addition to the program.

Claremont Graduate University was located a few miles from Chino in a residential area that featured ivy-covered brick buildings. The classes were expensive and typically had only six to ten students. I paid as much as I could and took out a student loan to pay the rest. (The loan took me about ten years to repay.) When it was time to select a topic for my dissertation, I decided to take a look at murderers. While working at RCC, I got to talk to the more-serious criminals, not like the ones I encountered at the diagnostic center. I came up with a series of questions to ask each murderer I interviewed. I made arrangements to have all the people committed to CDC for murder from Southern California assigned to my caseload. People committed to prison for murder from Northern California went to the prison in Vacaville for processing, and those sentenced to death went directly to San Quentin.

I interviewed more than three hundred inmates who killed one or more people and were convicted of murder with sentences from fifteen years to life, to life without the possibility of parole (LWOP) in prison. Some of those I talked to were purely evil. There was no doubt they belonged in prison, but the death penalty would have been a better solution.

By this time it was 1980. I had grown my hair longer than normal and sported a full beard. I must have had a strange look about me. Actually some of the inmates were scared to sit in my office for the interview. They said I had "Manson eyes" and that I asked difficult questions. I had started using the skills Al Martinez and the guys in my attack group at the diagnostic center had taught me. I rejected superficial responses. I forced uncomfortable disclosures. My questions were designed to make the inmates uncomfortable. Some of them would break down and cry, while others would get angry and hostile. Considering some of the inmates I agitated, it probably was a rather dangerous and foolish tactic.

It is difficult to comprehend the magnitude of the vicious and sadistic nature of some of these criminals. Though I spent about an hour in an eight-by-ten-foot room with each one, the only thing I knew about their crimes was written in various police and probation officer reports and what the inmate told me.

My office was along a hallway with about ten offices. Each counselor had an office with glass windows on the side that faced into the hallway. Correctional Officer Joe Reyna patrolled the hallway and also brought the inmates to the offices for their interviews. It was an ideal situation for me. I created a list of the inmates I wanted to interview the next day. They would show up one at a time and then go back to their cell when we were finished.

Occasionally one of "my" murderers was considered too dangerous to be housed on the main line, so I had to go down the corridor to the Palm Hall housing unit. On May 21, 1981, I went to Palm Hall to interview Roy Norris, prisoner number C-30231. I rang the buzzer at the door and was greeted by the correctional officer. He let me in and took me to the interview room. Norris was escorted in handcuffs and brought in to see me. I asked to have his cuffs removed—I still possessed some care and treatment ideas; behavior could be modified, people fell into crime through bad circumstances.

Palm Hall was an administrative segregation area where we housed gang members and high-profile inmates such as Norris. When we greeted the newly arriving inmates at the classification committee meeting in Palm Hall, we told each of them the unofficial rules. The sergeant would tell them, "We let all inmates on the yard at the same time. If you fight with another inmate, we will shoot you." The inmates felt they were entitled to fight with opposing gang members. Usually the inmate would ask, "What is the warning-shot policy?" The response surprised them: "The first warning shot will be in your head." We rarely had fights on the yard. Occasionally someone would test the policy. The occasional shootings would help keep the peace for a while.

Peace officers typically have the authority to use deadly force to stop someone from inflicting death or great bodily injury, even in the outside community.

Norris and Bittaker

Roy Norris was committed to prison for forty-five years to life for five murders, rape, and robbery. His crime partner, Lawrence Bittaker, had been sent to San Quentin following his death sentence. Norris had served a couple of years in the navy, during which time he completed a GED, and then he received a general discharge because of psychological problems. He said he used heroin while in Viet Nam but did not become addicted. Norris usually had been employed as a laborer or electronic technician, a skill he learned during a prior prison term.

Norris was arrested for attempted rape in 1969, but the case was dismissed due to lack of evidence. The following year he approached a young lady on the San Diego State College campus. After talking to her briefly, he hit her on the head from behind with a rock. After she fell to her knees, he held her head and bounced it up and down on the concrete sidewalk. Norris was classified as a mentally disordered sex offender and committed to Atascadero State Hospital. After almost five years in Atascadero, he was released to Los Angeles County on probation.

In less than six months after release from the state hospital, Norris approached a young lady walking home from Tony's Restaurant in Torrance after having an argument with her husband. He asked her if she would like a ride on his motorcycle and tried to give her a hug. At that point Norris grabbed her scarf and twisted it around her neck. He told her, "I am going to rape you." The victim was then dragged into the bushes and raped by Norris. He was found guilty by jury and sent to state prison on January 21, 1976.

Roy Norris ended up at the state prison in San Luis Obispo, the California Men's Colony (CMC). While there he learned a skill—electronics—met his crime partner, and planned his next series of crimes. As prisons go, CMC was a good place to do time. Prisoners could learn a trade, pick up some academic classes, and steer clear of the gang problems that plagued other prisons. Norris met Lawrence Bittaker during his vocational training classes, and they became friends. On a couple of occasions Bittaker helped Norris avoid problems with other inmates. They had mutual interests and would be getting out of prison within ninety days of each other. Bittaker was paroled in November 1978, and Norris in January 1979. While living at his mothers' house, Norris received a letter from Bittaker discussing some mutual interests and planned activities. They began spending weekends together, taking pictures of young girls in bikinis in the south bay area of Los Angeles.

Norris and Bittaker had put together a detailed plan while they were at CMC. The plan was to rape, torture, and murder a teenage girl for each of the teenage years: thirteen, fourteen, fifteen, etc. They purchased a 1977 GMC van with sliding side panel doors specifically so they could slide open the door, grab a girl, throw her in, and then close the door quickly. They named the van the Murder

Mack. They found a location out on a fire road in a remote area of the San Gabriel Mountains, above the city of Glendora. The prep work included walking around the beach area taking photos of girls. Over the next few weeks Bittaker and Norris picked up about twenty female hitchhikers, but did not harm them.

On Sunday, June 24, 1979, the two parolees were cruising along the beach area looking for a good victim. At 7:30 that evening they spotted a sixteen-year-old blond girl walking in the Redondo Beach area. She had attended a senior fellowship meeting at Saint Andrew Presbyterian Church and was on her way home. As she passed the parked van, Bittaker and Norris jumped out and grabbed her. They threw her in the van through the sliding doors and sped off with her screaming.

The young girl was taped up and taken to the fire roads in the mountains. After raping her, they decided to kill her. Bittaker pulled her out of the van and held her while Norris tried to strangle her. When he saw the look of terror in her face, Norris took his hands off her throat and threw up. He couldn't continue. She asked if they would let her pray, but they wouldn't stop. Bittaker tried to strangle her, but he couldn't do it either, so he cut a section of a coat hanger and gave it to Norris. Norris tried to twist it around her neck, but couldn't get it tight enough to kill her. Finally Bittaker was able to twist the coat hanger with a pair of vice grips tightly enough to kill the girl. They decided to throw the victim's body over the steep hills so that the animals would eat it and there would be no trace of her. After numerous mountain searches, her body was never found.

Two weeks later, on Sunday, July 8, 1979, Bittaker and Norris were hunting for their next victim. An eighteen-year-old blond girl was hitchhiking on the Pacific Coast Highway. Bittaker was driving, and Norris was in the back hiding under a makeshift bed. The Murder Mack with the sliding door stopped. The girl was offered a drink. As she walked from the back of the van to the front, Norris came out from under the bed and attacked her. There was a furious fight. She tried to fight off the bigger and stronger Norris, but she lost the battle. They taped her up and drove to the San Gabriel mountain area on a fire road above the city of Glendora.

They drove from one mountain area to another, stopping so each could rape her and take photographs. Bittaker jammed an ice pick through her right ear into her brain, then pulled it out and jammed it into the left ear. He then manually strangled her to finish off the job. Again they threw her body into the steep hills for the animals to consume. Her body was never recovered.

Eight weeks later, on Sunday, September 2, 1979, two girls, fifteen and thirteen years old, were hitchhiking at the corner of Pier Avenue and Pacific Coast Highway. The van with the sliding door approached the two girls as they sat on a bench at the bus stop. Norris rolled down the window and offered the two girls some marijuana. The side door of the Murder Mack opened, and the girls got inside and started smoking. After about five minutes went by, Norris struck the thirteen-year-old girl in the head with a sap that he had made the week before. As she tried to get out of the van, Norris punched her in the face and knocked her to the floor. While this was going on, Bittaker was struggling with the fifteen-year-old. The men gagged and taped up both girls.

This time the two murderers became even more sadistic. They again drove to the mountains above Glendora. For the next two days, Norris raped and tortured the fifteen-year-old girl, while Bittaker tape-recorded her screams of pain. They drove to the fire road where the other victims had been killed. Norris stood guard while Bittaker shoved the ice pick through her ear then strangled her with his hands—no coat hanger this time. Bittaker then yanked the thirteen-year-old victim out of the van and hit her on the back of the head with a sledgehammer then started strangling her with his hands. While Bittaker was gripping her neck, Norris took the sledgehammer and repeatedly struck the girl in the head. Both of the young girls were thrown over an extremely steep area for the animals to eat.

On September 30, a young girl managed to escape from the two murderers. She had been subdued by the two men using mace. After she was raped, she somehow managed to escape from the Murder Mack.

About 11:30 in the evening on Halloween 1979, the serial killers were hunting in the Sunland-Tujunga area of the San Fernando

Valley. A hitchhiking sixteen-year-old girl accepted a ride, getting into the van with the sliding door. Like something out of a horror movie, Bittaker and Norris grew even more monstrous. For the next two hours, they used pliers on her breasts and other body parts while Bittaker tape-recorded the event. During the torture, Bittaker proceeded to rape and sodomize the young girl while Norris forced her to perform oral sex. In order to increase her pain and their pleasure, Norris continually smashed her right elbow with the sledgehammer to make her scream more. Norris used a coat hanger and vise grips to strangle the girl until she died.

Becoming emboldened by the fact that they were not being stopped, Bittaker thought it would be interesting and fun to see the reaction of the press if they tossed the body out in someone's front yard. The mutilated body of the sixteen-year-old girl was dumped in the ivy at the front of a house in Sunland.

On February 9, 1980, a mountain search conducted by the District Attorney's office and the Sierra Madre Search and Rescue Team uncovered the partial skeletal remains of the thirteen- and fifteen-year-old girls. The partial skull of the fifteen-year-old girl still had the ice pick embedded in it. The Hillside Strangler serial killer had just been caught a few days before.

In between the murder events, Roy Norris met an old prison friend and started describing the crime spree he and Bittaker had been on. The gruesome stories must have been too much even for his prison friend. The information was passed on to the police, and some of the details matched the information provided by the young lady who had escaped the Murder Mack back in September. Once the police provided pictures of the two killers, the victim was able to make a positive identification. Bittaker and Norris were arrested for unrelated crimes and held without bail. During interrogation, Norris began unloading all the details of the murder spree, blaming Bittaker for most of it.

Norris worked out a deal in exchange for his testimony against his crime partner. The police found more than five hundred photos of girls the two had taken. Of the five hundred, there were nineteen identified as missing. Norris would tell investigators what happened to only five of them.

The case went to trial and featured a tape recording of one of the torture sessions. The jury was stunned at the horror. Lawrence Bittaker was sentenced to death. In addition, he was given a 199-year-to-life term, just in case his sentence was ever commuted. Roy Norris was sentenced to forty-five years to life in exchange for his cooperation in the case.

Having read the file, I was prepared to talk to Norris. He looked disheveled and had a wild, sad look in his eyes. My first question was intended to hurt him. I looked him in the eyes and said, "What the hell is wrong with you?" He stared at me a second then began to tremble a little. His whole body was shaking. I didn't know if I had made the right decision to have his cuffs removed. He didn't get up from his chair, so that was a good sign. He finally spoke. "I am an evil person. I should be killed. I wish I had gotten the death penalty. Can you help me get back to court so I can ask for the death penalty?" I didn't know what to say. He stopped shaking and looked drained.

Here stood Roy Norris: military service, high-school education level, considered cured of his sexual deviation by the state hospital, trained in electronics during his prior prison term, now in a room with me following a despicable monstrous crime spree that took the lives of at least five young girls. There are no words available to adequately describe this situation. Death by pressing or death by a thousand cuts[6] comes to mind—something torturous to gain some level of equivalence. But instead, all we are left with is forty-five years to life with a parole hearing around December 2008. As of July 2009, about thirty years after the first young girl was murdered, Roy Norris was housed at the Substance Abuse Treatment Facility in Corcoran. His crime partner Lawrence Bittaker is still at San Quentin awaiting execution.

Reading the events captured in the central file of Roy Norris and others like him changed the way I looked at the men who came to prison. Maybe not all of them were as evil, but there were

---

6 Pressing was an ancient method of torture or execution. Heavy weights or stones were placed on the subject's chest until a confession was secured or death occurred. Death by one thousand cuts was an old method from China in which the subject was cut with a knife many times in small increments. Death would occur, eventually.

a lot more of them who really needed to be in prison than those who might have been able to function in the community under some sort of supervision. People usually are in prison for good reasons, and some of those people need execution.

Lawrence Bittaker   *Roy Norris*

Avital

In February of 1982, I met Jehuda Avital, prisoner number C-42080. He was born in Tel Aviv, Israel. His father was a mechanic for the police department in Tel Aviv. Avital quit school at the age of fifteen and spent a couple of years in the Israeli Army. The army didn't work out for him, and he spent some time in jail for desertion before coming to the United States illegally by way of London in 1979. He wanted to open up a barbershop but instead ended up selling drugs. Avital stayed with a couple from Israel he had known since childhood, Esther and Eliahu Ruven. They had been drug dealers in Israel and were applying their trade in Los Angeles then.

According to Israeli police records, Avital was arrested first at the age of fifteen for stealing a car. He was involved in several property crimes including theft, burglary, fraud, and possession of drugs, but had no history of violence.

Danny Myers was a regular customer of the Ruvens'. He bought cocaine from them. The Ruvens, Zakaria, Komerchero, and Avital maintained an apartment in the San Fernando Valley on Sherman Way. The group kept scales, testing, and packaging equipment at the apartment to facilitate their drug business. They would test, weigh, and package the cocaine, then make their deliveries. They were dealing heavily in transactions of five to ten kilo quantities of cocaine, purchasing the drugs for about seventy thousand dollars per kilo. Avital's duties were to deliver the cocaine as well as collect money and provide protection. Zarkaria was responsible for purchasing the drugs from the connection, and Komerchero was considered an employee.

The Ruvens were certain Zakaria was ripping them off and responsible for the seventy thousand dollars they owed the connection. The group held a couple of heated meetings in September 1979. The Ruvens complained that Zakaria and Avital were cheating them on cocaine deals, and Zakaria and Avital had the same complaint about the Ruvens. Mr. Ruven asked Komerchero to take the place of Zakaria and Avital, and at the same time Zakaria and Avital asked Komerchero to replace the Ruvens.

On October 3, 1979, Avital was in Las Vegas, staying with Julie and Lane Conley. He received a phone call from Zakaria, who was in Los Angeles. Avital asked Lane to buy some .22-caliber bullets for him. Avital took the bullets and a bowie knife with him and drove to Los Angeles in the Conleys' car, arriving the next day. On October 5, Zakaria, Komerchero, and Avital drove to the Bonaventure Hotel in Los Angeles. Since the Ruvens didn't trust Zakaria or Avital, it was up to Komerchero to get the Ruvens and bring them to the Bonaventure. On October 6, Komerchero, Avital, and Zakaria bought three suitcases from the May Company department store. When Komerchero got to the Ruvens' apartment, he told them about a meeting at the Bonaventure. Mr. Ruven was anxious to go. When Komerchero indicated they would be doing some freebase cocaine, Mrs. Ruven insisted on going along.

Avital hid in the bathroom in room 2419. He was dressed like a butcher, wearing white shorts, slippers, an apron, and rubber gloves. His gun with a silencer, boxes of bullets, and the bowie knife were ready. Zakaria opened the door, and the Ruvens came in with Komerchero. Avital emerged from the bathroom in his butcher outfit and began shooting. Mrs. Ruven's face was covered in blood. There was blood everywhere. Mr. Ruven ran toward the door but Avital stabbed him with the bowie knife. He then dragged Mr. Ruven into the bathroom.

Mrs. Ruven was lying on the floor bleeding in the main part of the hotel room. She asked Avital what would become of her three-year-old daughter. Zakaria was busy moving around the hotel room and seemed to be wearing different clothing each time he came into Mrs. Ruven's sight. She was half conscious. The sound of chopping and crunching was emanating from the bathroom as Avital dismembered Mr. Ruven. Each time Avital emerged from the bathroom he had a big smile on his face and a body part in his hand.

After finishing with Mr. Ruven, the butcher proceeded to rape the half-conscious and bleeding Mrs. Ruven. He then took her into the bathroom and dismembered her body. While cutting up the bodies, Avital displayed the genitals of each victim

After the job was finished, Zakaria gave Avital some trash bags to package the remains. There wasn't enough room for all the parts in the three suitcases they bought, so Zakaria had to go down to the luggage shop in the hotel to purchase Samsonite luggage. They cleaned up the room, during which time Avital became hungry. Komerchero went to the closest McDonald's and brought back some food. Everyone changed clothes and left in the car Zakaria had left on the street for Avital and Komerchero to use. They drove off with the body parts packed in the suitcases stored both in the car trunk and in the back of Zakkaria's truck. All the suitcases were dumped in trash bins. Zakaria, Komerchero, and Avital then left Los Angeles for New York.

I had called Avital in for an interview after I had already spoken to his crime partners Zakaria and Komerchero. He sat in the chair in my office. My office furniture was arranged so that my desk did not act as a barrier between the inmate I was interviewing and me. We sat about three feet apart, facing each other. He was a little fidgety and had his jaw clenched. My first question was, "Mr. Avital, the probation officer's report says you are a member of the Israeli Mafia. What is that about?" He became agitated. "I am not a member of the Mafia. That report is full of lies." Next question. "The report also says you butchered a couple of people and stuffed the parts into some suitcases. What the hell is that about?" Avital began to tremble in his seat. His face became red and distorted with anger. "That report is full of lies. I am appealing my case."

I was trying the attack group tactics that had worked before, but I didn't seem to be getting anywhere. "Well, the fact is, two people were butchered and their body parts were put into suit-cases then in dumpsters. Why do you think someone would have done that?" Avital spurted out, "Maybe they ripped somebody off, and he got very angry. Now where are you going to send me?" He was getting agitated again. "Well, I think Folsom will be a good place for you." On February 1982, seventeen days after arriving at CIM, Avital was transferred to Folsom State Prison. He didn't stay there long, moving to protective housing at Soledad the next year then on to the security housing unit at San Quentin before going back to Folsom in 1989. Last I checked, he was at the Level IV prison at Kern Valley, and was prisoner number C-42080.

My research on murders was wrapping up. I had finished all my classes, qualifying exams, language skills[7], and work on my dissertation. To my surprise, the majority of the murderers thought the death penalty would be a deterrent if it were actually used. My dissertation defense was successful, and I received my PhD in criminal justice in January 1984. By the end of that year, I had been asked to help with the activation of a new computer system the department was developing called the DDPS (Distributed Data Processing System). I moved to headquarters in Sacramento and started working as a data processing analyst.

I was surprised that when I first left CIM, I felt a lot lighter. I never noticed the weight of working in a prison until I moved

_____

7 The language skills requirement can be met by passing statistics or computer programming languages. The more traditional method was to be proficient in a foreign language.

to a more normal environment. I helped design a couple of the statewide automated systems then moved over to the Institutions Division to develop some personal computer-based systems. Even though I had left the prison environment, I still felt more comfortable around "prison people," which I attribute to having in common with them some sort of shared experience.

The new job enabled me to help the institutions automate several functions. My work garnered accolades from the wardens, but at the same time made me an enemy of headquarters executives outside of Institutions Division. Primarily because I was able to get things done quickly and efficiently without going through normal bureaucratic procedures. I enjoyed doing battle on behalf of the prisons with the executives, but eventually my operation was toppled by headquarters power manipulators. I worked in the Inmate Classification Services Unit for a while, then got a call from Jim Tilton, the deputy director of administrative services. He needed my help with some personnel automation problems. I dropped my interest in regaining peace officer status[8] to again do battle with headquarters executives on behalf of the prisons. It was a familiar and comfortable role for me. I knew I was good at it and also knew I would probably one day be shot down by power manipulators.

Years later I would address the subject of the death penalty in a paper that was posted on Pacovilla.com:

The Death Penalty in California: Bogged down by legal maneuvering and judicial fine-tuning What do murderers think? Is it like cold peanut butter? January 11, 2011

According to a recent *Los Angeles Times* article, with 717 condemned inmates on California's death row, the legal tug-of-war over capital punishment is expected to intensify, especially with incoming Governor Jerry Brown and Attorney General Kamala Harris, both known to oppose executions on moral grounds.

---

8 Correctional counselors are considered peace officers. This designation provides enhanced pay and retirement benefits.

Both, however, have said they will uphold death sentences in their new jobs.

According to World Lingo, the first execution at San Quentin was Jose Gabriel on March 3, 1893, for murder. The first hanging at Folsom was Han Chin, also for murder, on December 13, 1895. A total of 215 inmates were hanged at San Quentin, and 92 were hanged at Folsom. The first people to die in the San Quentin gas chamber were Albert Kessell and Robert Cannon on December 2, 1938. They were involved in a failed escape attempt at Folsom State prison in which the warden was killed. Three more people had their death sentences carried out within two weeks. Up until 1967, 194 people were executed by lethal gas, including four women. The last person was Aaron Mitchell on April 12, 1967.

The California Supreme Court ruled in *People v. Anderson* that the current death-penalty laws were unconstitutional and oversaw the commutation of 107 death sentences in the state in 1972. In a 1976 decision, the California Supreme Court again held the death penalty statute was unconstitutional, as it did not allow the defendant to enter mitigating evidence. An additional 70 inmates had their sentences commuted. The latest change of method came in January 1993, when the lethal injection was given as a choice for people sentenced to death. David Mason chose to die in the gas chamber, because he wanted to suffer for his crimes. In 1994 lethal injection became the default method. The first person executed under these new laws was William Bonin in 1996. Since California reinstated the death penalty in 1977, 13 people have been executed, but 56 others have died on death row of other causes, including 14 of suicide (through October 25, 2007).

In February 2006, a de facto moratorium on capital punishment was enforced in California, as the state was unable to obtain the services of a licensed medical professional to carry out the execution of Michael Morales. An injunction made by the Ninth Circuit Court of Appeals held that only by a medical technician legally authorized to administer IV medications could carry out an execution. The lethal-injection procedure, if wrongfully performed, could lead to suffering for the condemned, potentially constituting cruel and unusual punishment.

A review of a logbook maintained at Folsom State prior to moving the operation to San Quentin reveals that the time between death sentences imposed by the courts and execution was relatively short, sometimes less than one year. Due to various court decisions, the time spent on death row awaiting execution has been growing significantly. The US Bureau of Justice released a report in December 2010, *Capital Punishment, 2009—Statistical Tables.*

- Average number of months between sentencing and execution increased by 30 to 169 months from 2008 to 2009.
- From 1973 to 2009, 73 inmates in California prison died while on death row awaiting execution, while 13 were executed during that time period.

According to the **Sacramento Bee** article on January 1, 2011, *The Conversation: Can California confront costs of the death penalty?* :

- Up until the 1970s, California executed about a dozen murderers each year, with an average wait of three years between sentencing and execution. The average delay in the U.S. is now 12 years. In California, it is 24 years.
- The biggest reason for the delay in California is that the demand for competent, experienced death penalty lawyers vastly exceeds the available supply. The size of the available supply is directly related to the economics of practicing law in a state like California. More than 40 percent of the 713 inmates on California's death row are still waiting for

the appointment of a lawyer to handle the habeas corpus reviews to which they are constitutionally entitled.

- Most of the $54.4 million we spend each year for capital appeals and habeas reviews comes out of the state budget.
- The most recent polls show 70 percent of voters support the death penalty.

There is little reliable research available regarding the death penalty that is not the subject of heated debate. Some feel it is cruel and unusual punishment. In Louisiana in 1946, Willie Francis was "executed" in the electric chair. There were voltage problems, and he survived. Afterward Francis stated the experience "tasted like cold peanut butter." He was later successfully executed. It is difficult to determine what the impact of the possibility of the death penalty is on individual criminals. Did people convicted of murder consider the possibility of imposition of the death penalty prior to committing murder? A study in 1983 included interviews with more than 325 men convicted of murder in California who were sentenced to prison for life terms. Here are some of the highlights:

- 28 percent had served a prior prison term.
- 43 percent of the victims were strangers to the murderers.
- 77 percent of the murderers were appealing conviction.
- 56 percent said they were guilty.
- **47** percent **of the murderers felt** *implementation* **of the death penalty would be an effective deterrent**, 45 percent did not, and 9 percent didn't have an opinion.

Having a long time pass between the crime and the punishment weakens the impact for both the victim's family and the murderer. A grisly murder captures the headlines, followed by news stories, then before you know it, ten years have passed and the murderer exists on death row, sometimes entertaining a group of fans through the Internet. The entire legal system suffers. Legal costs mount, and the taxpayers are forced to devote large sums of money that could better be spent elsewhere. In addition, appeals that go on for years are hindered by chang-ing law-enforcement techniques, public and media interest, and the memories of people involved in investigations.

It would be very helpful if the length of time between the imposition of the death sentence and the execution were at least reduced to the 1984 national rates. Any death-penalty reform efforts should be directed toward shortening the time between a death sentence and an execution.

5

Headquarters — Rise and Fall

It was the summer of 1997. Having finished most of the assignment that brought me to admin division, I began to look for other things to keep me busy. I was working as the chief of our personnel automation section located at the old Mayflower building at Twentieth and J Street in Sacramento, across the street from the local free weekly newspaper, the *Sacramento News and Review*. It was a tree-lined street in an old residential section that bordered on the busy J Street restaurant and boutique section. We were close to the local drug program that doled out methadone, so there were criminal types that hung around, sometimes sleeping in Dumpsters. One afternoon when I went for a walk on J Street, I heard a woman's voice coming from the vacant lot I was passing: "Don't look." By shouting that out, she drew my attention. I saw a disheveled, dirty-looking woman in her fifties squatting next to a tree with her pants down. She looked at me and shouted, "What's the matter with you? I gotta take a shit." Just what I needed to see.

In this job I was responsible for the automated systems used to keep track of all the positions and pay for the staff in the department. I always had a difficult time keeping busy at work, so I would look for things to do other than my assigned duties. Most of the

49

time I came up with what I thought were some good ideas; unfortunately, not everyone saw things the same way I did. Ideas would hit me when I was walking around the neighborhood or reading a book, or just talking to someone. After getting an eyeful on my walk, I started thinking about combining information from our two automated systems and putting together a report looking at trends. I thought the concept was rather simple but was not aware of the turmoil it would raise.

The information I gathered included recent trends for sick-leave use by correctional officers and overtime paid. From the data I put together, it looked like the use of sick leave was increasing and overtime pay was also going up, evidently to pay for correctional officers to work in place of those calling in sick. Since most positions in the prisons are staffed twenty-four hours a day, seven days a week, someone had to fill in behind those who called in sick. The staff working the overtime shift earned time-and-a-half pay. The way I looked at this trend was fundamentally different than the way most people saw it. When correctional officers work in inmate housing units, they become familiar with the inmates they supervise. They know where they work, where they hang out, who their friends are, and when their behavior is different than normal. These subtle observations can help avoid problems like fights, drugs, or escape attempts. When the regular officer is out sick, the relief officer is not familiar with the inmates or their routines. This is a time when inmates may do things they wouldn't do when the regular officer is there.

I put together a pretty good report and sent it to Deputy Director Jim Tilton. I had worked with Jim for about ten years, and he had promoted me to my position in personnel. Jim was a good man. He was intelligent and made good decisions. Unfortunately, at this time, there was some turmoil at the top. Somehow one of the other deputy directors, Teresa Rocha, was elevated to a position higher than Jim. Rocha was in her early forties and rather diminutive—a little more than five feet tall and maybe one hundred pounds—and had a reputation for having two personalities: sometimes she was very pleasant; and other times, a terror. The more power she had, the more her evil side was on display.

As far as I was concerned, these were just stories. I had not witnessed any of her behavior. She had worked as the warden at Folsom State prison before, but had never worked in any custody positions on the line.

Within a few days of my submitting my report to Tilton, Rocha had him fired. She didn't like having people around who were smarter than her or knew more than her. If she had to use someone like that, she wanted to keep him at a distance. I think she knew she was inferior to Tilton in every way, so she had him removed from his deputy director position. Jim left the department and went to work at the department of finance. His departure was not handled well by Rocha and company. To replace Jim, Rocha selected Steve Kessler. Kessler also was a very competent and intelligent man. I don't think he knew what he was getting into. Rocha selected Wendy Still to be her assistant. Still was a brutish person known for her sloppiness and logorrhea. She was a hard worker, but she would talk nonstop about her topic of the day. She usually had a minimal understanding of her subject matter and liked to slant things to fit her misguided ideas.

Steve and I got along great. He liked my ideas about the sick leave and overtime data, and he talked to Rocha about it. In February 1999, Steve and I were sent on the road to deliver the data to all of the wardens, then all of the administrators in headquarters. Rocha had me do a presentation at a cabinet meeting, and Director Cal Terhune had already approved it. We took Rick Burrows, the budget officer, with us. The first stop was going to be CRC for all of the southern prison wardens, then a stop in Fresno for the central prisons, and Sacramento for the northern prisons. Steve and Rick called it the road show. If it was a show, I guess I was the main act.

It was great going back to CRC after more than fifteen years. I got to see Gari Hall. She and I worked together at CIM back in 1984. Gari was now an associate warden and later became warden at CRC before retiring. I also ran into Bud Prunty, who was now a regional administrator, supervising all of the southern prison wardens. Bud thought the presentation of the data was terrific. The entire road trip was a success. We had only one detractor. When we did the presentation in Sacramento for the northern wardens, Ed Alameidia did not like what he heard. Alameidia was the warden at the Deuel Vocational Institution (DVI). He had the reputation for running the prison under budget and the tightest fiscal controls. He was considered to have the best fiscal operation—until everyone saw the data I had.

DVI was not the best-managed prison, if you were looking at sick leave and overtime management. Turns out, they were only average. This disturbed Alameidia to no end. During a break in the meeting, he cornered Director Terhune and told him the data I was presenting was not accurate. In fact, he said that it was "dangerous." He cautioned Terhune, "What if the union gets hold of this information?" The union supposedly pulled Terhune's strings on a regular basis. The seed was planted. Within a matter of days, Kessler told me Rocha wanted me to stop providing the data we had taken on the road show. She also wanted to know why I was providing the information. This was bizarre, since she had authorized the road show. Steve said he couldn't explain her behavior, but the show was over. I was told to just drop it.

Coincidentally, the state auditor's office was conducting an audit regarding fiscal issues in CDC. They often conduct audits at the direction of the legislature. Many times they were at odds with the areas under the jurisdiction of the governor's office. I was asked to provide personnel data to the auditors. What a stroke of luck! They were interested in sick leave and overtime. They asked me to pull some data from our automated systems. I thought about the "just drop it" instructions and decided to take a different path this time; I offered my report with the data I had taken on the road show. The auditors looked at the report and said, "This is exactly what we are looking for." This was another in a series of bifurcation points for me. Nothing would ever be the same. Sometimes you reach a fork in the road, and you just take the path you know is not the easiest. It would have been easy for me to "just drop it." But that day I didn't feel like it.

The state auditor blasted the department for its management of sick leave and overtime in a public report. The report was titled, *California Department of Corrections: Poor Management Practices Have*

Resulted in Excessive Personnel Costs. The report described how we were wasting millions of dollars in taxpayer money by not managing our sick leave and overtime. Once this report was public, it was easy to trace the information source back to me. On January 10, 2000, Rocha had Steve move me away from the office at Twentieth and J. She wanted to make sure I no longer had access to the data available through the automated systems. Steve said, "She just has this thing—she wants you, Richard Krupp, physically located over here next to my office." I had to move to the headquarters office at 1515 S Street and be in an office next to Steve so he could watch me. By this time, Steve had been verbally abused by Rocha on a regular basis. He was assigned a "special project." He described the project and told me I would be working with him. Once I heard his description, I told him, "I've heard this story before, Steve; Rocha is going to fire you." Steve looked surprised. "No. I am working on a very important special project." I told Steve I would be glad to work with him, but repeated that he was going to be fired soon.

Steve went to talk to Director Terhune and was told he was not going to be fired. Terhune was not one known to be restricted to a strict interpretation of the truth. Within two weeks Steve was fired. He was shocked. I felt bad for him. Neither Steve Kessler nor Jim Tilton before him should have been subjected to the experience of being "Rocha-ized" as it became known. I was left alone with no work. This is not a good position to leave me in if you are managing a corrupt operation. I decided to put together a statewide employee survey. This would go out to all forty-five thousand CDC employees regarding their opinions about management and various other subjects.

Not fully understanding my operation, Rocha thought that keeping me away from the automated systems would keep me away from the data. To keep busy I decided to continue collecting sick leave and overtime data. I still had contacts at Twentieth and J. The people I worked with liked working with me and continued to provide me with data. I continued to update the state auditors so they could see that the problem was getting worse. Because of some changes to the contract with the union, the officers could now call in sick, then work the next day at time and a half. This small move increased the sick leave and overtime rates by one third.

On April 20, 2000, I was asked to meet with Wendy Still. She had a former warden, George Ingle, and former chief deputy warden Bobbie Reed in her office when I went there. Ingle had the demeanor of a marine, and Reed was a large, matronly-looking woman. Ingle wasn't the brightest bulb on the tree, and Reed had a PhD from what our research office considered a substandard school. Wendy said I would be reporting to these two retired annuitants. The department often hired back administrators who had recently retired. The retired person could collect 90 percent of the salary they earned when they retired and a second paycheck for about the same amount. I packed my things and moved to the fifth floor of the south building. Ingle gave me an office right outside his.

After moving my things, I met with George. I told him I was in the middle of the staff survey and should have that wrapped up within sixty days. He told me my assignment was to write the department's response to the state auditor report. How ironic. I had provided the information that the auditor used to publically blast us for mismanaging sick leave and overtime; now I would be involved in the response. George said that they had made some significant operational changes recently at Wendy's direction that had really turned things around. Sick leave and overtime was now under control. I asked if he could get me some information on the changes that had been made and some data that we could use to do a before-and-after comparison. George said he would get the information the next week.

I read the materials describing the changes that were implemented at Wendy's direction. Knowing how the sick leave and overtime system worked, it did not seem like the changes they implemented would make any difference, but the data would tell me for sure. I went through the automated data and then met with George. "George, I went through everything you gave me, and it looks like things are not improving, they are getting even more out of hand. In fact, the overtime has increased to $105 million annually, more than thirty percent higher than it was before."

George was stunned. He looked like someone just told him his best dog died. "That can't be. We have made a bunch of changes."

"Sorry, George. Things are not what you were expecting. Maybe we can tell the auditor that we are trying some things out to see if we can improve? Looking at the changes that were implemented, I would say it is not likely things will improve." George went away mumbling something about talking to Wendy about this.

The next day George came to my office with a sneaky look on his face. He sat next to me in a chair almost facing me, with about two feet of space between us. He had a half smile as the words uncomfortably seeped from his lips, "Can you make it look like the sick leave and overtime is getting better?" Here it was: another fork in the road. From my previous experience dealing with the CIM inquisition and the road show experiences, I knew I had two choices: If I did what George was asking, I might get back in the good graces of the administration. They would see me as an asset again. If I refused to participate in the scheme, I would be going down the rabbit hole, not to see the light of day again. That moment felt like the riot at YTS when I was moving in slow motion. With only a split second of hesitation, I spoke: "George, I can't tell the state auditor the rates are improving; that's not true. Even if you could fool them into thinking you had things under control, how could you then ask for assistance to fix something you have said is no longer broken?"

George did not like my answer. "So you are refusing to follow a direct order?"

"I will not help you lie to the state auditor." There it was: the path was chosen, the conditions set, and there was no way back. As George walked away, I knew I was going to be subjected to bolts of lightning from the highest parts of the organization. In my opinion, Ingle, Still, Rocha, and Terhune were incompetent administrators. I was not going to help them; in fact, I was going to do battle! Stand or fall, it was me against the CDC administration. I had to prepare for a protracted fight with an uncertain outcome.

The first thing I wanted to do was confront Still, Rocha, and Terhune with the information. Maybe they did not fully understand the data? Maybe they would relent and truthfully respond to the auditor? George got someone else in the office to twist and manipulate the data to make it look different. At one point he even added vacant positions into the calculations to make it appear the rates were down. Of course vacant positions do not call in sick. Even with all of the manipulations, the data still did not come out they way they wanted. I met with my three opponents on August 21, 2000, to discuss the data and the untruthful response that Terhune was about to sign and send to the state auditor.

Wendy described her interpretation of the data and the official CDC response. It was obvious to me that she did not have a background in statistics. She tried to describe the trends and how she arrived at her conclusions. Though I brought documentation to support my position, Rocha and Terhune did not look at it. They listened for a few minutes then once again suggested I "just drop it." Terhune said he was sending the response as written by Wendy. He got up and went to the corner of his office juggling his keys that he kept in his right front pocket. I told him, "I know what you are going to do next. You are going to send me to a hole somewhere with no work to do." He smiled and juggled his keys as I got up and left.

I went back to my office on the fifth floor of the south building. Bobbie Reed approached me there and said that since I had "a different philosophy about the data" they didn't need my help anymore. I asked her what that meant. "If you mean that an increase is actually a decrease, then yes, my 'philosophy' is different. I don't think up is actually down." Bobbie asked me to give her my key to the office. I guessed this was symbolic, since I didn't actually use the key to get in. I kept the key in my desk and never actually used it, since the office was always open when I was there. I gave her the key then fired off my first shot in the upcoming battle.

I got on the phone and called my contact at the state auditor's office. "John, this is Richard Krupp. I have some information for you." I told him about the data, the response, and the meeting I had just had with the big three. I told him I would put all of my supporting documents in the mail to him, and he could decide for himself if up was down. It felt good. My battle was with people who were miscalculating my resolve. They were taking me lightly, and it would come back to haunt them. I can't really explain what drove me to take a stand. Maybe I was fed up with all the bullshit. Maybe I thought I could force the incompetent buffoons to change.

I wrapped up the staff survey and put together a report that described the more than thirteen thousand responses I received. Since I had asked all the employees to tell me what they thought about a number of issues, I felt I owed it to them to read every response. More than five thousand people took the time and effort to provide detailed written comments in addition to filling out the survey. Reading everything was something that would prove invaluable in the days to come. It would be a great weapon in the battle, something the other side could not match. I had the time to read and understand everything that was thrown my way. Information was read, digested, analyzed, and understood for later recall. I also began keeping a record of everything that happened during the day, anything in some way significant. This was another great weapon that was unmatched by the other side.

My fall from grace was taking turns in strange directions. On August 28, I got a call to meet with Frank Renwick about my current job status. Frank was an average-looking guy, other than the bright red hair. He called me into his office and asked me almost apologetically, "Where do you want to work? You are no longer needed on the fifth floor." I told him I would like to go back to my old job in personnel automation at Twentieth and J. Frank said that was not an option; my old job had been eliminated. I asked what my options were, if going back to my old job was not one of them. He said he didn't know. "Rocha just asked me to ask you where you want to work."

"If I can't go back and you can't tell me what the options are, then I have no response."

Frank tried to make it easy. "How about this? Where do you *not* want to work?" I should have seen it coming. "I don't want to work in the Research Office." I did not want to work with the guy in charge there, John Berrachochea. He had some odd ways of doing things.

On September 8 I was asked to meet with Liz Mitchell. She said, "You are going to work in the research office." There it was.

The other side decided all they needed to do was move me to an office where I did not want to be, and I could start my punishment. When I met with John, I found out that even though I was a second-level supervisor, I would not be supervising anyone, and I would have no real assignments. According to personnel regulations, my classification required at least three subordinate supervisors, each with at least three subordinates.

I was given an occasional research proposal to read and write a one-page summary on. The work I was given in the research office kept me busy one or two hours a week. Some of my free time was occupied by researching information I needed for the house I was building. My wife, Calla, and I had completed a weekend course on general contracting. We decided to purchase some property and have a house built. This required me to read construction plans, contracts, and budgets. I had plenty of time at work to do this.

Having almost forty hours a week to fill became a growing problem. Some days I would come to work, and no one would even speak to me. I could go three or four days in silence. Since I had about 170 hours of idle time to fill each month, I had to figure out what to do. Working on my house-building project at work didn't seem right. With little substantive contact, I found myself falling asleep at my desk, and apparently no one would notice. I started going on walks each morning, dividing the days into segments. Start work at seven thirty, walk about a mile for a morning coffee break at nine, sit outside by the fountain at eleven, look at Internet sites from noon to two, then rest until four o'clock before going home. After a month or two, it started getting to me. There didn't seem to be an end in sight. I applied for other jobs, but no one would hire me; I was marked. When I went for interviews, I found the people on the interview panels were the ones involved in the retaliation. I had to break out of the cycle.

Since I did have occasional assignments that involved reviewing research papers or proposals submitted by colleges, I began reading books related to the subject areas of the research. If UCLA submitted a paper regarding drug-abuse treatment, I would read a book or two that would provide some background information for my evaluation. It was rather odd. I would read the twenty-five-page research paper then read two 250-page books before writing a one-page evaluation. This made for a very good evaluation and reading kept me busy for hours. I found myself walking to the Tower Records bookstore on Broadway every week to pick up a couple of books. This is the same store the Unabomber used to frequent. I read somewhere that he liked a book by Joseph Conrad called *The Secret Agent*. I picked up a copy. This was unusual for me, since all the other books I was reading were nonfiction.

My daily walks and book reading would take my mind off my dismal situation for a while, but there wasn't an end in sight. It had been months since I landed in the research branch. I had read about seventy-five books related to submitted research by now. The subject areas had expanded to include economics, complex systems theory, and even quantum physics. I had continued my Internet searches and one day stumbled across a website that featured California State Senate hearings. CDC was always getting in some sort of predicament related to poor management practices. I found the minutes from a hearing regarding whistle-blowers, featuring a hearing conducted by Senators Jackie Speier and Gloria Romero. The door to the world of whistle-blowing had cracked open.

I read the transcripts from the hearing on February 28, 2001. The words of Senator Speier stuck in my head: "Despite the savings of taxpayer dollars that might be attributed to the courage of whistle-blowers, their reward, more often than not, is to be afforded the status of outcast or victim. Job demotions and ridicule are the unfortunate legacy of someone who dared to report an improper activity. As a whistle-blower, if I had only a four percent chance of having my retaliation claim substantiated, I'd be loath to blow the whistle too." My situation sounded bleak. It was nice to have someone interested in my plight in a conceptual way, but I had never dealt with politicians before. Should I write or call the senator? According to the words of Senator Speier, I was in for more trouble.

I needed to do more research. I began checking out websites for the State Personnel Board, the Bureau of State Audits (BSA), and the Office of the Inspector General. At first I tested the waters. I called the BSA after reading a section of the California government code that said they would investigate complaints of retaliation associated with whistle-blowing. The terms *retaliation* and *whistle-blowing* were almost foreign to me. They didn't feel right when I spoke them out loud. I just thought of myself in terms of trying to do the right thing and being subjected to punishment at the hands of incompetent people. If only I could get all of the information to the right person, everything would be corrected. That was how I viewed my situation. Certainly someone within CDC would realize that I had done nothing wrong, and I could be restored to my previous status. Reaching out to BSA was just to get information in case all of my efforts within CDC failed.

I called the BSA hotline to discuss my situation. A few minutes into the conversation I was told, "We don't actually investigate complaints; we refer them to the state personnel board."

"But the government code says you investigate complaints."

"I know it does, but we refer them to the personnel board for investigation." This sounded strange, but was typical government runaround. Next I called the state personnel board. After explaining my situation to the person on the phone, I was told, "We don't actually investigate; we review written complaints."

"So I write up the complaint, send it to you, you look at it, then make a decision?"

"Yes. We also give the department an opportunity to respond to the complaint." I was referred to another section of the government code and provided information about the process. I was told that since I worked for CDC, I had another option; I could file a complaint with the Office of the Inspector General (OIG). The rules about this option were in the California penal code.

The first thing I needed to do was review the government code sections relative to the Whistle-blower Protection Act and the penal code sections related to whistle-blowers and the OIG. I had the time and interest to take on the new reading assignments; all the while I kept reading more books, applying for jobs, and hoping I would get my sentence commuted or a pardon from some

CDC official who would call me up and say it had all been a mistake, a momentary lapse of reason. I read more books.

After reading all the code sections and the complaint rules and requirements, I decided to take a two-pronged approach. I would file a complaint with both the SPB and the OIG. The OIG might actually conduct an investigation, while the SPB would do a "paper investigation." I wrote up the complaint and held it for a while, trying to decide if I really wanted to go down another rabbit hole. According to the Senate hearing transcripts, people suffered even more retaliation after they filed complaints. I was still having a hard time seeing myself as a "victim" of retaliation, a "whistleblower." There was an interview coming up. Maybe I had one last chance to get out of the hole I was in.

I was scheduled for in interview for a position in our offender information services branch. They were looking for someone with my skills, and I was the only one left on the hiring list they could select. It seemed like a perfect way out. The interview was scheduled after I responded to the letter of inquiry. I arrived early and waited in the office on the fourth floor. I heard my name called and looked up to see Liz Mitchell. She was the one who sent me to work in the research branch after I had told Frank Renwick I did not want to work there. This didn't feel right. I went in and sat across the desk from Liz. She asked a few questions that I answered. She seemed disinterested in my responses.

The following week I learned the position I interviewed for would not be filled at this time. There would be a new exam so that a person could be selected. Evidently I was not wanted. When I found out they were going to all that trouble to conduct a new exam so they wouldn't have to hire me, I finally realized there was no way out of the hole as long as I was dealing with people within CDC. I had reached another fork in the road. I decided to move forward and become the "whistle-blower" and "retaliation victim." The words felt strange, but I would try them on like a new set of clothes. The role fit, but the labels felt uncomfortable.

I put together a well-documented complaint. On August 6, 2001, I walked to the State Personnel Board office and submitted my complaint then walked to the mailbox and dropped in the complaint for the OIG. Once the complaint with all of my supporting documents dropped into the bottom of the blue mailbox, it made a thud that brought me a sense of relief. I was no longer waiting and hoping for something to change; I was on the offensive. It was my declaration of war. At this point I had no assistance in this fight: no lawyers, no advocates, and no work friends. On the way back from the mailbox I walked past the state capitol building.

6

Harsant Tantsi

I went to visit with a man I had met a couple of months before. Harsant Tantsi lived at a senior residential facility at Thirteenth and N streets across from the capitol in a building that looked like an old hotel. Harsant used to sit out front in the mornings waving at people walking by. He was around eighty-five years old and sat in a wheelchair. Surgery a few years back to correct a bone spur went awry, leaving him unable to walk. This man had competed in the United States Olympic trials with the likes of Jesse Owens; he ran track with gold medalist Eddie Tolan, but now couldn't stand up. His dignity, sense of humor, and memory like a steel trap made him stand out. We would spend about an hour each Monday through Friday talking about politics, sports, and days of future past. I confided in him like I would have my father if he were still alive.

South Bend's finest: Tantsi's track team back in Depression-era Indiana.

Evidently Harsant used to work for Frank Sinatra as a chef and general assistant. He would tell me stories of late-night dinners he cooked for Frank and his friend Dean Martin. The only similar stories I had to tell involved being on the stage crew in grade school back in Detroit and setting up the bench that Stevie Wonder sat on when he played the harmonica and sang at our school Christmas show. He was in the blind class at Fitzgerald school a couple of blocks from where I lived.

As I approached the Park Place senior facility, Harsant spotted me and greeted me with his usual broad smile that was more like a smirk sometimes. He always looked like he had some secret that he wanted to keep to himself. This time he appeared to sense that I had something special to share with him. "What's new?" he said. "I just sent in my complaint to the Inspector General and the Personnel Board." Harsant was very familiar with my troubles at work. "Good. Give 'em hell." He seemed to take some special pride in my actions. Harsant came to this country with his family in the early 1900s. His father was a minister in Africa and was a founder of the AME (African Methodist Episcopal) church.

The other big news to discuss today was the softball game from last night. Harsant loved to hear me describe my games. The team was mainly comprised of guys much younger than me. Both of my sons and their friends were on the team known as the Replacement Players. We formed in 1994 around the time of the major league baseball players' strike. While most of the players on our team were in their twenties, I was approaching fifty. "We won last night. It was a close game, 25-4."

"Doesn't sound too close. Sounds like you pounded them pretty bad."

Slow-pitch softball games can get a little lopsided. "Both of my kids hit homeruns, and the old guy struck out a couple." He liked to hear me talk about my sons.

We didn't talk about Harsant's family much; he never mentioned any kids. I had the feeling he was reluctant to talk about any kids he might have. Today I decided to broach the subject. "Do you have any kids?" There it was, out on the table. We usually didn't beat around the bush when we were together.

"I have a son, but haven't seen him in a while."

"How long is a while?"

"About forty-seven years."

"Forty-seven years? How old is he?"

"About forty-seven." Harsant spoke with a lump in his throat but, as always, with an air of dignity. "When Junior was born, I was trying to get my spells under control. People thought there was something wrong with me, and my wife thought it would be better if I stayed away from the baby."

"What was wrong with you?"

"No one knew what was wrong at the time; so I left. I moved away and lost touch. Later I found out I have epilepsy. My wife died later, and I never saw my son again."

As his words hit my ears and sunk in, I felt a gnawing in my gut. How could this be possible? How could I possibly help? What am I supposed to do about a childhood tragedy? "Have you tried to find your son?"

"Yeah, but no luck."

"Would you like me to help you get in touch with him?"

Harsant paused and thought for a brief moment. "If it's not too much trouble; yes." This man, who never asked for anything, was kind of asking me to help find his son.

7

Investigations

Once the State Personnel Board gets a whistle-blower complaint, they conduct a review of the paperwork and decide whether there is enough information to warrant an investigation. This is the same type of process utilized by the Office of the Inspector General. The differences in the two investigations are substantial. The SPB review is really only a review of written submissions by the parties involved, while the OIG actually conducts an investigation with recorded interviews by peace officers. There didn't appear to be a formal coordination between the two agencies, though the OIG has a more direct reporting relationship to the governor.

I received a letter from SPB indicating my complaint met the requirements and had been accepted—case number 01-2338. This letter meant I would soon be identified as a whistle-blower. The department would know that I had come out of the woodwork and was on the offensive. According to the rules of engagement set forth in the government code, I had certain protections from retaliation while my complaint was making its way through the review process. I knew the department would try to cover their tracks as much as possible, but they would not be able to keep up with me if I kept focused and continued to document things as they occurred and read everything I could that had anything to do with my case or the applicable laws and rules. All I had to do was stick with it. I thought I had thought of everything.

The SPB sent a letter to the department indicating I had filed a complaint. This must have pissed a lot of people off. I was able to check calendars for some of the managers I identified in my complaint and noticed there were a few meetings scheduled to discuss my case. They included one of the department attorneys, and I took this to mean they were a little concerned.

On August 29, 2001, I received a letter from the OIG indicating they had accepted my complaint as well—case number 01-108. Now things were going to get even more interesting. There were elements of my case that could lead to criminal findings. I knew that this would draw out the tendency to start pointing fingers and looking for someone to blame. This was something the department did well. The rats were starting to scurry. I read more books.

I received a meeting notice from Barbara Sheldon, one of the department attorneys, and Paul Kopf to meet regarding my complaint. When I arrived at the meeting, there was one other attorney as well. Sheldon acknowledged my complaint and indicated the department had done nothing wrong intentionally, and they were trying to find a place for me, since my old job had been eliminated. There was a certain amount of arrogance in the discussion. The department assumed they could operate as if they had more autonomy than they actually did. They underestimated their opponent and did not really have the time or energy to devote to the case. I, on the other hand, knew the strengths and weaknesses they had. They did have almost unlimited legal resources, but they were vulnerable on other fronts.

Coming into the meeting, I had prepared by looking into position vacancies and surprised the attorneys. "First of all, I believe the department has hindered my ability to promote. I am on two promotional hiring lists, but can't get a promotion." Barbara responded, "The department hasn't done anything to hinder your ability to promote, and we can't just promote somebody just like that."

"Then put me back in my old job in personnel."

Barbara shot back, "As I mentioned, your old job was eliminated."

I was quick: "If it was eliminated, then why is there a bulletin posted indicating the job is now open?" From the reaction of the attorneys, I could tell that someone had lied to them. They made a move I would see many more times. Lawyers drive down a road they have laid out and assume there won't be any surprises. When they reach an obstacle, they try to drive around or over it. When they reach a dead end, they ask for a time out to regroup. "We will have to get back to you on that."

The department decided not to cooperate with the SPB investigation. Instead they sent a letter to SPB on October 23, 2001, indicating they hadn't done anything wrong but they were working diligently to find me a suitable position. They provided no supporting documentation to refute my claims. It appeared they were taking the SPB investigation very lightly, probably because they were focusing efforts on the OIG investigation. I was called in for a meeting with Chief Deputy Director Kathy Kinser. She told me she wanted to get me "on the road to recovery." I asked her what I was going to recover from, but she had no response.

Kathy said she had spent hours last night going through department job announcements on my behalf and had found a perfect job for me. She told me to meet with Ernie Van Sandt and get the details. After talking to Van Sandt, I discovered he didn't know what job Kathy was talking about. He didn't have a job for me. When I confronted Kathy about the discrepancy between what she told me and what Ernie said, Kathy did that lawyer thing: "You must be mistaken. I don't recall the exact conversation." I told her that I read through all the job announcements that she claimed to have read through on my behalf and could not find anything similar to what she described. Again she replied, "You must be mistaken."

At this point I was sure no one was going to help me. The SPB was taking too long, the OIG was waiting for the SPB to finish, no one was going to hire me, and I was in my eighteenth month doing nothing at work for forty hours a week—but still reading books.

When people feel they have nothing to lose, they sometimes do things that are not rational. I decided that I would no longer participate in this bad dream. I would just work somewhere else. I called Jim L'Etoile from the department's Office of Substance Abuse Programs (OSAP). "Jim, I have worked as a counselor for inmates with drug problems and am very familiar with drug-treatment research. I would like to come over and work in your office." Jim was a little confused. "I don't have any vacant positions." I responded, "That's OK. I can start tomorrow."

I didn't care about any state rules regarding position authority, funding, SPB rules, or anything else. I just told people I decided to work in OSAP, and someone would have to figure out how to deal with everything else. On January 14, 2002, I started working at OSAP as a supervisor. Miraculously, all of the necessary paperwork was completed in one day. Two days later, the SPB issued the Notice of Findings on my investigation. Coincidence? I don't think so. They found that I was retaliated against for disclosing information on sick leave and overtime problems. The findings would be final in thirty days. However, the process became even more complicated. If I wanted adverse action to be taken against the retaliators, I would have to file something called a Request to File Charges with the SPB. If I wanted any compensation for the retaliation, I would have to file a lawsuit.

I had actually helped the department out by going to work in OSAP. They made it look like they found the job for me, thus ending any ongoing retaliation. On my birthday, just before the Notice of Finding was scheduled to become final, CDC filed a petition asking for a hearing before an administrative law judge. I read the Petition for Hearing they filed and provided a response. As usual, CDC had done a very poor job reviewing the facts and explaining their weak position. The SPB blasted the department, stating they had "failed to submit any information to support its bald denials of wrongdoing." My well-documented complaint was no match for CDC. The Petition for Hearing was denied, and the Notice of Findings was final on April 3, 2002. I read more books.

All of the information from my SPB action could now be a part of the OIG investigation. While the struggles with the CDC and

SPB were going on, I was also working with the OIG. On October 19, 2001, Deputy Inspector General David Faingold interviewed me. I drove to the inspector general's office not knowing what to expect. I had never been interviewed by a peace officer and didn't know how to prepare. I brought some of my documentation with me. David was a former police officer and carried himself like a by-the-book cop. He wore a badge on his belt and had a handgun in plain sight.

David explained the process and told me the interview would be recorded. He placed me under oath, and the tape recorder started. At first, we just went over my work history and other non-threatening things. I wasn't sure if this was necessary information or just to get me comfortable or off guard. I didn't see David as an advocate, just looking for information to help him decide where to go next. I had gotten used to telling people about my plight. It actually helped by talking about it. I didn't have anything to hide. I just went from the head and heart and let the facts speak. I made it clear that I didn't know if what was being done to me fell into the category of illegal behavior, but I knew it didn't feel right.

The interview went on for about three hours; a couple of times, the recording device had to be stopped to put in another tape. I provided a long list of people I thought had information that would shed some light on what was happening. It would be up to the OIG to determine whom to interview and in what order. After the interview I felt relieved. A weight had been lifted, and I felt lighter. I left David with a box of documents and promised to get additional information he requested.

Field interviews were conducted between December 2001 and February 2002. More than a dozen people were interviewed by the OIG. All of the interviews were recorded, and most of them were transcribed. On May 23, 2002, the OIG issued a Report of Findings that stated, "The report sustains, in whole or in part, allegations of retaliation committed by Wendy Still and Teresa Rocha." A copy of the report was sent to the State Personnel Board with the following admonishment: "Penal Code Section 6129 (c) mandates that an employee who intentionally engages in acts of reprisal, retaliation, threats, coercion, or similar acts against another employee as described in Penal Code Section 6129 (a)(2) 'shall be disciplined by adverse action as provided in Section 19572 of the Government Code.'"

The day the report came out, I received a phone call from David Faingold. I was walking to work that morning and had just crossed the street by the state capitol. "Hi Richard, this is David Faingold. The report just came out today. Are you sitting down?" I walked to the cement bench next to a monument for fallen peace officers. "OK, go ahead." "There are findings of retaliation against Rocha and Still, but nothing against Mitchell or any others." This was even better than the SPB findings. There had been an in-depth review of my supporting documentation and extensive interviews by the OIG. This was very satisfying. Certainly things would get better now. I had prevailed in both investigations. The department would finally admit defeat and let me out of the hole they had shoved me in.

Over the next two years, trying to get the Department of Corrections to take some form of discipline against the people who retaliated against me would be like trying to nail Jell-O to the wall. Trying to get hired off a promotional list would be even more difficult. I think the findings of the OIG really stung CDC. I had stirred the demons and now faced their full wrath. As with most large organizations, there was a large legal defense team available. The department hired contract attorneys to represent the top two culprits, Rocha and Still. The Department of Personnel Administration would represent some of the respondents, CDC would supply legal assistance, and the attorney general would take the lead on the case. At one point I counted twenty-two lawyers involved in the case representing the department.

Recognizing that the odds were against me, I looked for an attorney who had successfully battled CDC in the past and did not require a lot of money up-front. My wife did some research, and we contacted a few law firms, including one of an acquaintance. Everyone, including my acquaintance, turned me down—except

John Houston Scott. He had successfully taken on the department recently and won a large settlement for some CDC employees. John agreed to drive to Sacramento from his San Francisco office on a Saturday and meet my wife and me. We met at Java City on Eighteenth and Capitol. John is a medium-sized man with piercing bluish eyes and a bright smile. He sat down with us over coffee and listened intently. I had told the story so many times by now that I could remember dates, looks on faces—every detail. John agreed to help.

It appeared that the CDC decided to take the path that involved various legal delay tactics and hide-the-ball maneuvers. We filed a lawsuit to try to force their hand. Maybe the department would buckle under legal pressure? I never felt very comfortable with the legal maneuvering. It seemed to be like playing a game involving threats and dares. I felt like I had just gone up and down a lot of turns and switchbacks on a train going through a mountainous road. The end of the track was no longer in sight. Maybe that is what lawyers do. They want you to take your eye off the ball—get distracted.

The game of Discovery came into play. Each side demands to see certain unspecified documents. I was never sure if this was a red-herring game or an attempt to bury me in paper that no one really wanted or took the time to read. I wasn't even aware that the game was designed to be a ruse. I actually provided all the documents I was asked for through the process. When my demand for documents was answered, I learned a new tactic. My document demands were found to be "vague and ambiguous." I was a quick learner, so I changed the format of my demands to mimic the format used by the CDC. Eventually they changed tactics. Instead of saying my demands were "vague and ambiguous," the CDC decided to overwhelm me with documents so voluminous that no one in their right mind would want to read through the thousands of pages.

Once again the CDC miscalculated. I spent hours utilizing the critical reading skills I had developed to read all the documents the CDC gave me. By this time I developed the ability to read page after page of just about anything considered nonfiction and retain the highlights as well as pick out the weaknesses. For me, departmental operations and legal issues relative to whistle-blower retaliation made for a simple read compared to quantum physics, pharmacology, economics, and constitutional law. I would spend hours reading through documents, highlighting in yellow the significant points and jotting down notes. I was essentially preparing a legal brief. My wife would review my brief and help fine-tune the package, then we would send it to my attorney.

It was quite an impressive operation. The CDC would supply the documents, I would read through and apply legal standards I was familiar with, then John Scott would put together a legal argument. I am certain the legal team assembled by CDC had put together a similar assembly line, but they lacked something very important. Everything I was doing was personal. It was directly related to me, not just part of a job. The opposition had many cases they were juggling, and mine was more of an irritant than something personal. I had placed myself in an interesting position. I felt I didn't have anything to lose. The CDC had already destroyed my career advancement possibilities, and I was not doing anything that could lead to my termination, so I felt I could state my piece: stand or fall. People who feel they have nothing to lose are dangerous. They don't react to stress, as one would expect.

Then I found it: the smoking gun, so to speak. Sifting through a mountain of CDC-supplied documents one day, I came across a page with handwritten notes on it. It didn't seem to belong to the rest of the papers. The notes laid out the cover-up strategy of the trio of culprits, Rocha, Still, and Mitchell. The notes indicated a strategy: blame someone else, claim nothing happened, state ignorance. It also indicated there would be a campaign to get the OIG to change the findings in their report. Each of the three culprits were designated certain roles in the scheme. There was also a note indicating the trio was going after the transcripts from the OIG interviews to help them mount a defense—amazing stuff!

At some point the period of discovery ran its course. Now the CDC wanted to depose me. The deposition process could also be characterized as an inquisition. John explained the scenario to me. I would be in a conference room with the person from the attorney general's office across from me, the two hired contract attorneys, and about a dozen of the people I had named in my complaint. John said he would be sitting next to me but could be only of limited assistance. This was an opportunity for the opponents to practice intimidation and assess how I would respond in open court. How well did I know my material? How much grace under pressure was I capable of? To me it would be like pitching in a softball game.

To prepare for the upcoming deposition, I read through all of the yellow highlighted documents, my notes, and my log of events. I also read through the penal and government codes that were related to my situation. I spent hours and hours preparing. I was ready. John advised me not to bring anything with me, because any notes would be subject to discovery.

I met John in the morning for coffee. then we walked to the tall brownish building by the library. We took the elevator to the eleventh floor and the office of John Atkisson. As we entered the conference room, it was as John had described it. There was a large table with a lot of people I knew sitting with gloomy looks: Cal Terhune, Wendy Still, Jim Libonati, and several others, along with all the lawyers. John Atkisson, his partner, Sandman, and the AG Glenda Reager were in the room. There was also a stenographer in the corner. John and I sat at the end of the table with the opposing counsel. All of the "observers" were filling the remaining seats. After standard pleasantries, the game began.

I could tell by John's reaction that I didn't handle the first couple of questions very well. It reminded me of first-inning adjustments I had to make if I walked the first batter. We took a break, and John gave me a pep talk. Not knowing the rules of engagement, I had been a little hesitant and needed to be more aggressive in my responses. John told me to lean into the opponent. Throw some inside pitches or hit the corners.

My first opportunity came against Glenda. She held a document in front of me and started asking questions, but wouldn't let me read the document. This was a trick to get me to guess at some of the content and then show inconsistency between my recollection and the actual document. I might recall a certain date, for example, but be off by one day. When she asked me a question about the document, I told her I could answer the question better if she let me read what she had in her hand. She tried to intimidate me, but I refused to go along with the game. "Let me see the document, or move on." She began to tremble. Her face was getting red. "You are refusing to answer the question?" For the fourth time I responded, "Let me read the document, then I will answer your question." Glenda stared at me for what seemed like minutes. She was red-faced and visibly shaking. Her trembling hand finally moved toward me and with great disgust released the document from her tight grip. It fell to the table in front of me. I tried not to grin as I slowly reached out and lifted the paper from the table. I slid it toward me and turned it around, unsure if she would slap my hand before I got it.

As I read the document, I noticed it was a memo that was written about some remotely related information about the sick leave and overtime data. I easily explained Glenda's intentional misrepresentation of the memo. I felt as though I had dispatched the leadoff batter with a weak grounder back to the box. By now I found myself able to ignore the distractions from the observers. Their looks of disgust, their heads shaking from side to side, and their emphatic note-taking, did not concern me. I was in a zone. All I could see was the lawyer in front of me: like the batter and me, we were staring at each other. Now it was time for the big hitter to enter the box again.

Atkisson was up to bat. He had knocked me around a little in the first inning, but that happens to me often. It takes a while for me to feel my way around and get in a comfort zone. This time Atkisson was going after the retaliation events. The line of questioning he chose put me in a position to take some pokes at him. He kept starting his questioning with "Mr. Krupp." He was trying to paint a picture of a person who lacked credibility. I stopped him mid sentence and told him, "From now on call me Doctor Krupp!" He looked startled. First he was a little angry that I had interrupted his train of thought; then he looked a little amused. I usually didn't use my academic credentials in a formal way. "OK. Doctor Krupp." Atkisson proceeded.

The opportunity arose to introduce the smoking-gun information. I indicated that there was a concerted effort to blame someone else. Atkisson was at first amused at the response. "Where on earth did you come up with that information?"

"It was in the second box of documents your office sent to me as part of discovery."

Atkisson was stumped. He looked around the room and at his co-counsels. "We need to take a short recess." The words were spit out of his mouth as if he had tasted something bad. He was irritated. Once again my strength, reading everything and remembering most of it, had come in handy.

John and I went out into the hallway and talked. I could tell he was elated with my performance. He was almost giggling with delight. I asked, "Did I do OK?" John was so excited. "OK? You were great." I could tell that he wanted to be in the mix. A weakness had been found; John probably could have run a truck through the breach. I was not a capable attorney, but I knew how to confront inmates and ballplayers; lawyers weren't much different. There would be more battles, and it would carry over to the next day.

The second day of deposition battles saw a couple of people absent from the crowd. Wendy was no longer at the table, and, more interesting, John Atkisson was not to be seen. His partner Sandman had replaced him. She lacked Atkisson's arrogance and caustic approach. Now that I knew the process and the tactics, I felt very comfortable. It was going to be very difficult for the opponents to shake me. I knew my materials and the weaknesses of the other side. Instead of just responding to questions, I was going to interject some things I wanted to say. There may by objections, but I would be on the record. I would use the court reporter as a scribe for my position. Any time they gave me a slight opening, I would push through.

An opportunity opened up when I was asked what I expected my supervisor to do when I brought the retaliation to his attention. In this case the supervisor in question was Jim Libonati. I had told him about the retaliation on several occasions. Since I disclosed the retaliation to my supervisor, it was his responsibility to protect me. "It was his responsibility to protect me from retaliation."

"Where did you get that from?" responded the AG. It was written in policy and government code. I kept hammering that point in and got a lot of spectators sitting back in their seats and giving me a disgusted glance while they moaned in disagreement.

Everything was going well until the break. I went out in the hallway to call the voicemail on my cell phone that had been turned off during the deposition. I had one message. As I listened, I heard my mother's voice. She sounded different. "Richard, this is your mother. Can you call me please? It's your sister, Debby; she's dead. Please call me; I don't know what to do." I had two sisters. Debby was the youngest at forty-seven and had some problems in the past with prescription drugs. My mother's voice hit me like a punch in the stomach. I don't know which was worse, the news of my sister's death or the sound of my mother's pain. My mother needed me.

Without telling him why, I asked my attorney if I could reschedule the rest of the deposition. He looked at me like I was crazy. "This is going really well. You don't want to let them regroup. Besides, there will be more delays. Why do you ask? We are almost done." If I told John, he would pull the plug, and we would have to start over. My mother had called about an hour ago. I knew she would be calling my other sister next. I called.

My mother explained that Debby had been found dead in her apartment by a neighbor after she didn't show up for work. The cause of death was not yet known. My mother wanted me to be with her as soon as possible. She lives in southern California, about four hundred miles from me. I told her I would be there soon. I held my feelings in check and went back into the conference room. It was difficult to concentrate on the questions while having my sister and mother occupying my thoughts. I held up through most of the questions, but by the end of the session I was finding it very difficult to keep my mother and sister from moving to the front of my thoughts.

I couldn't control it anymore. "Look, I just found out my sister died, and my mother needs me. I think we are done here." I felt like I had just unloaded a heavy weight. Everyone in the room was surprised and a little shocked. John looked at me with concern and told the AG to wrap it up. She indicated we were done for the day and expressed her regrets. I moved out of the room and made some phone calls. My wife and I would fly out of Sac metro and head to Burbank airport, getting us to my mother's house that evening.

8

Spotlight

On March 23, 2004, I hit another bifurcation point. Things were changing again. I was sitting in the audience at the California State Senate, waiting to testify at a hearing on my situation. I had met with Senators Jackie Speier and Gloria Romero a few months back and talked about my situation. Senator Speier is a remarkable person. The first time I met with her was June 19, 2003. I had written a letter and received some e-mails and phone calls from Chief of Staff Richard Steffen. He was a tall, slender man in his late fifties. Richard was intense, intelligent, and very perceptive. He and Erin Ryan were the people I talked to, for the most part. Erin was the daughter of former Congressman Leo Ryan. She was tall, compassionate, and also very sharp. I was really impressed with Senator Speier and her entire staff. I would meet several times in her office at the capitol over the next couple of years.

The two senators were planning some hearings about the prison system, and they were looking for some examples to help them bring some issues out into the open. They talked to me for about an hour in the small, cramped office on the second floor of the state capitol. I described my situation as I had done many times before. Senator Romero listened intently, but had a look of suspicion. Senator Speier had both a look of skepticism and compassion. I expected the skepticism and suspicion; after all, my story sounded bizarre to most people, especially the part about reading books all day. By the end of the meeting, I felt that I had at least made a connection with Senator Speier. She asked me to follow up with some additional documents.

Richard Steffen called me a few days later and asked if I would be willing to testify at a Senate hearing. He was more aware of the significance than I was. To me it just sounded like an opportunity to tell my same ongoing story to more people; everyone would listen, shake their heads, then go about their business. Nothing ever changed for me, just different books to read. I told him I would testify and asked when the hearing would be. It sounded like there would be two or three hearings, but the agendas were not yet set. One of the first hearings included a guy named Max Lemon, an associate warden from Folsom. He was the star witness. I attended the hearing on January 21, 2004, to find out what I was in for. It was quite a show. The hearing room was a large auditorium with a large number of people in the audience and a group of dignitaries center stage, with news media crawling all over the place. I had never seen anything like this. There were cameras and microphones in front of people, behind people, out in the hallways, everywhere. You could feel the tension. I sat about fifteen rows back behind Lemon. Senator Speier and Romero were running the show and seemed completely in their element. They were in control. Lemon, on the other hand, was trying to pour a glass of water from the pitcher sitting on the table in front of him. His hands were shaking so much he was spilling as much water on the floor as he was into his glass.

Lemon was trying to describe a situation involving a riot at Folsom State Prison back in 2002 involving the Mexican Mafia. Max was accusing another associate warden at Folsom of assisting the Mafia. Lemon had told a reporter, "We must report crimes, whether staff or inmates are involved. And the same laws must apply to both. No one can be above the law. If we are to stand for the truth as a peace officer, the truth must be told." It was quite impressive. Max had also asked for protection. There were peace officers assigned to protect him. I am not sure why, but he had a security detail. It was going to be something. I could tell why the hearing was scheduled without me on the agenda. My situation would sound comical compared to this.

The hearing was going along with questions from the senators, gasps from the audience, and tears from Lemon. Something didn't go smoothly when they got to the videotape of the riot. During the fights and stabbing taking place on the Folsom yard, there was a camera shot of Lemon. It looked like he was having an altercation with an inmate during the riot. The only problem was that the inmate was lying on the ground, and Max could be seen kicking the inmate. This little misstep did not get past Senator Romero. She began asking some questions, and Lemon started getting flustered. A one point he began sobbing.

My first hearing came March 22, 2004. This time I was the star witness following State Auditor Elaine Howle. I had taken the bus to work that day as usual and wore a dark suit. I was well prepared. I knew everything I wanted to say, but had only a general idea about what questions would be asked. I was not exactly nervous, but not comfortable either. If I stumbled, would they eat me alive? Would people be sympathetic? There were a lot of cameras and reporters around, but I wasn't sure if they were just covering another hearing or if they were actually there to hear what I had to say.

I brought along a general outline of what I wanted to cover, so that I wouldn't forget anything, and a copy of a response to my employee survey that I thought might be a good example to show. After Elaine Howle was finished talking about employee discipline, it was my turn. Senator Speier called me up and started with some opening comments. One of the first things she asked me was how many books had I read at work, since CDC would not give me any real work to do. When I responded "Two hundred and six," I could feel the audience sigh and the reporters take notes.

When she had mentioned that the spotlight would be on me, I guess this is what the senator meant. I was able to describe in what was probably too much detail the cycle of retaliation and the general lack of attention to detail CDC had shown. Just when my presentation started to hit a lull, I started talking about the employee survey I had completed, and I pulled out the example I had brought. I held up the survey form, which had written on it in big letters, "FEAR OF RETALIATION—REFUSE." The cameras flashed.

An embarrassed-looking Jeannie Woodford, newly appointed CDC director, was called to respond to my testimony. It was odd that she and the new secretary, Rod Hickman, had taken up the position of my opponent after Ed Alameida had been removed from the director position. He had been pummeled through a series of hearings Senators Speier and Romero conducted. New laws had been passed, and CDC had been changed to CDCR. The *R* was for rehabilitation. Woodford promised to look into my case.

There were news articles the next day in the *Sacramento Bee* and the *San Francisco Chronicle* that gave me some hope that resolution was near. The picture of me holding up the survey response was featured in many news articles across the country. This added a leg of support to go along with Senator Speier, the OIG, SPB, and a growing following in the CDC as well as other state agencies. People would stop me in the hallway, on the street, and in airports to provide messages of support. It was something I had never experienced before.

The next day I got a call from Pia Lopez, who worked in the editorial section of the *Sacramento Bee*. She wanted to meet and find out more. Evidently she was in attendance at the hearing. We met a few days later at the newspaper offices. She wanted information that would support my assertions about the sick leave and overtime as well as the retaliation claims. I provided her with the tables of data, OIG, SPB reports, and so on. She wanted to spend some time looking the materials over.

On March 28, 2004, an editorial ran in the *Sacramento Bee*: "Krupp's complaint; Governor must protect whistle-blowers." This must have aggravated CDC and Governor Arnold Schwarzenegger. The governor's office constantly monitored the media to see what was being said about him. CDC was unable to put a good spin on what they were doing. The department wanted an SPB hearing to try and overturn the SPB decisions. The department was also trying to get the OIG to change the report they had issued.

I found out that the CDC had gotten Inspector General Steve White to change the report. It looked like they had decided to have Teresa Rocha take the fall for everything, taking Wendy off the hook. However, the SPB hearing could proceed if I dropped the lawsuit. I agreed. By now my legal bills were mounting, but I wanted to keep going.

We had an administrative law judge managing the hearing at an office at 660 J Street in Sacramento. John Scott represented me, while a group of lawyers represented the group of Rocha, Still, and others. One attorney from CDC headquarters slept during most of the proceedings. The highlight for me came when we called Rocha to the stand. She was asked to explain how she knew what other people discussed with the OIG during their confidential interviews.

She sat in her chair with her legs so twisted that she looked like a corkscrew. She bunched her five fingers together in her right hand and poked them at her forehead again and again. It was as if she were trying to pull a good answer from her brain. When that failed, she admitted that a box containing the transcripts from the OIG interviews had been delivered to her home. When instructed that possession of those documents was improper, she claimed she had them but had not read them.

Evidently, when the OIG provided the transcripts to the CDC so that adverse action could be taken against executive staff, the documents were instead turned over to the retaliators so they could mount a defense in the SPB case. Rocha had to testify for hours. It was a pleasure to see her squirm. I thought of all the pain she had inflicted on Kessler and Tilton before me as well as many others. I hoped she felt our pain.

When the Senate hearing was scheduled for the confirmation of Rod Hickman as secretary and Jeannie Woodford as director, I made known my intent to appear at the hearing and oppose their confirmation. Nettie Sablehouse, Appointments Director for the Senate Rules Committee, contacted me to find out what I would be saying. I emailed an outline of the testimony I would deliver. At the hearing, Senator Burton was the chairman. He couldn't keep Jeannie Woodford's name straight. He kept calling her Woodard or some other derivation. Odd, since she reportedly named the San Quentin library after Burton's brother.

I was called to the table to sit next to Woodford to make my comments. I brought a package with me that I left for her. It contained a book: *Integrity,* by Stephen L. Carter. Hickman sat slumped in a chair behind us as I spoke, then I left as both were confirmed.

In late July, the CDC did something so stupid the dam broke. My wife and I had planned a visit to see my mother in Southern California. On this occasion, my wife would travel a couple of days ahead of me. I opened an official-looking letter addressed to her from the CDC. When I read it, I could not believe what it said. Evidently the CDC had initiated an investigation into my wife's use of a state vehicle. The investigation was initiated nine days after I testified against Hickman and Woodford.

I wanted to write a letter to someone who could make them stop, but who? Should I write to the newspaper? To Senator Speier? The OIG? I thought about it for a while. Maybe no one would care? Maybe nothing would work. Then I figured it out. The department was struggling with the possibility of a federal receivership. It was like an open wound subject to infection. Perfect. No one else thought it was a good idea, but it felt good to me. I wrote a letter to Judge Thelton Henderson regarding the stepped-up retaliation. He was considering whether the department needed to be managed by a federal receiver. There were a number of areas of concern, including employee discipline and inmate medical care. I thought it unlikely that Henderson would respond to me, so I sent a copy of my letter to the *Sacramento Bee* editorial section. I did this against the advice of my wife and my attorney. I was tired of waiting.

The next day the *Bee* ran excerpts and some comments as an editorial. It was like setting off an explosion. They followed up the next day with the complete text of my letter; there were more news articles and buzz at the state Capitol. Senator Speier wanted to talk to my wife to find out how she was doing. I can only imagine the rats scurrying in CDC headquarters. What a bunch of buffoons! I hoped they couldn't sleep at night.

At some point CDC buckled. They couldn't withstand the onslaught. Someone was forcing the end to the battle—someone outside CDC. They agreed to a settlement conference. We met with a mediator, my attorney, his colleague, and CDC representatives. The ordeal lasted several hours. Back and forth, back and forth. In the end they offered me $500,000 and agreed to destroy the bullshit investigation they initiated on my wife. No sooner had I signed off on the documents than the department gave a whole file of information to a reporter from the *Sacramento Bee.*

While I was riding home on the light rail, I got a call from Andy Furrillo, a *Bee* reporter with details about the settlement. He had an article almost completed that he would run the next day disputing the nexus between my confirmation hearing testimony and the investigation on my wife, based on information the CDC had provided. Fortunately, I had copies of e-mails I had exchanged with State Capitol staff, showing they knew in advance what I planned to say at the hearing. Andy corrected the story before running it.

9

Blowing the Whistle Again

After I got the $500,000, I paid the required taxes and also purchased a condo in Canada. We had vacationed in British Columbia often and liked the area. At work I settled down in my OSAP position, managing the substance abuse program contracts. At first I felt relaxed. CDC had hoped I would retire and stay out of their business, but I didn't want to.

My section of OSAP monitored how the contractors delivered drug-treatment services and how they spent taxpayer money. Someone in the legislature had been convinced that the drug counseling would cure the inmates, so to speak, and reduce their recidivism rates. A study regarding a program run by the contractor Amity was used to substantiate the success of the "therapeutic community" model they were using. I made it a habit to read any research studies and books regarding drug treatment. A study conducted by the US Bureau of Prisons had pointed out the flaws in the Amity study.

The model used by OSAP included nine months of in-prison drug treatment followed by 120 days of "aftercare" in the community while on parole. The programs were in place at many of the prisons, with about nine thousand beds dedicated to drug treatment all together in the prisons and thousands more in aftercare. Each two-hundred-bed prison program cost about one million dollars a year, and the aftercare beds cost anywhere from $47 to more than $100 per day.

Each in-prison program was run by one of the "big six" contractors; Walden House, Phoenix House, Mental Health Systems, Centerpoint, Amity, and Civigenics. The aftercare contracts included three of the same contractors plus Westcare. These companies would hire a lot of former drug addicts as counselors and pay them close to minimum wage. The group meetings and so forth were scheduled for about twenty hours each week. The aftercare programs were located throughout the state.

In the three years I worked in OSAP, I recall only one contractor other than the "big six" who successfully won a bid. Odyssey House won the bid for a program at the California Men's Colony after the prior contractor refused to bid, wanting more money than the budget called for. Odyssey House did not work out, and the contract was cancelled. This contract was replaced with a program run by prison staff.

The OSAP office maintained a cadre of analysts who would conduct site visits, checking for contract compliance. The office also had a group of correctional counselor level threes stationed in each prison program and an assortment of parole agents to monitor the aftercare operation. A couple of times each year, meetings were held with an assortment of representatives from contractors and CDC staff. Then entire operation cost well over $100 million annually.

Since I had read extensively a great deal of research dealing with drug treatment, I collected various measures of performance and wrote a few papers. One of my first papers, published in a small academic journal, reported results of the entire group of inmates participating in the programs. It looked as though the recidivism or return-to-prison rates for the program participants were better than the general CDC recidivism rates. Things looked promising.

However, UCLA published a report annually for the legislature regarding the programs at SATF. The study was well designed and included a control group. Each time the study was updated and released, the findings were the same; the non-treatment control group had lower recidivism rates than the drug-treatment group. I began analyzing the data more closely with some input from the researchers at UCLA. It appeared there was a difference between aggregate data and comparable group data.

A common design flaw in this kind of research was evident. The aggregate data included an almost equal numbers of male and female inmates as well as a large number of civil addicts. These were not equivalent groups. When the comparisons were made with similar groups, the findings were somewhat alarming. In almost every case, inmates participating in prison drug-treatment programs did worse than those who did not participate. In addition, those who participated in an in-prison drug-treatment program and went on to participate in aftercare did even worse.

I did come across data regarding a small group of inmates who completed the in-prison programs and 180 days of aftercare with remarkable results. Their return-to-prison rates were very low. I asked staff to identify these inmates so that we could interview them and find out what contributed to their success. After scrutinizing the data more closely, we found that, for the most part, the group of inmates who completed the program including 180 days of aftercare were not real. Apparently information submitted by the contractors for data collection was faulty.

We found that apparently some inmates were counted as being in aftercare when they were still in prison. Some were counted in aftercare when they were parolees at large. The "success stories" were in fact just an illusion. This brought up another question. If the contractors were submitting invoices for aftercare people who weren't actually there, were we paying for them? Turns out we were.

As I began to report these findings at quarterly meetings and write reports, people began to get angry. I developed a survey to help us determine what the inmates thought about the drug-treatment programs. The responses provided a number of suggestions to improve the outcomes. The primary suggestion was to make the program voluntary. About half of the inmates said they either didn't have a drug problem or didn't want drug treatment. If only volunteers were placed in the programs, about half of the contracts would not be needed.

I wrote a paper regarding the survey findings and suggestions. Following publication I was told by the OSAP chief not to write any more papers. How strange. Here were some ideas to save taxpayers millions of dollars and improve operations, but further discussion was forbidden. As it turns out, the staff-run program at CMC was based on voluntary participation. This program had the best outcome data.

In what became a common finding, inmates who participated in drug treatment and aftercare following their release from prison actually did worse than those who did not participate in drug treatment at all. No matter how you sliced it, these findings were consistent. Even the study conducted by UCLA over several years on the CDC programs at the Substance Abuse Treatment Facility in Corcoran found this to be the case.

The usual response from CDC regarding this sort of information was to figure out a way to change the results of the studies or to hide or discount them. On one occasion I was asked by Jim L'Etoile, the OSAP chief, to change outcome findings. I found this rather amusing. I asked him, "Do you know who you are talking to? I'm the guy who blows the whistle and prevailed in a confrontation with the CDC." He regrouped and asked another OSAP employee to help him.

Based on faulty stories of success and legislative advocates, money was constantly being thrown at drug treatment. Another bright idea was Drug Treatment Furlough (DTF). This program would allow prison inmates to serve part of their sentence in a community-based facility very similar to the aftercare facilities. It was projected this would save money and show improved recidivism rates. Contractors were paid for "dedicated capacity." This enabled them to bill the department for their beds whether they had inmates to fill them or not. We were actually paying more than $100 per day for each empty bed. In addition, some of the "empty" beds were housing county inmates for a fee. The department had estimated there would be about 1500 inmates to start the program at any one time or about 4500 annually. However, the estimate was based on an "OBIS run." The antiquated computer program was utilized to kick out a list of DTF-eligible inmates based on the established criteria.

Unfortunately, there was always a big gap between the computer eligible list and the actual list eligible after the inmate central files were reviewed. I liked to call this gap the "OBIS funnel." I suggested that you take the OBIS numbers—in this case, five thousand—and assume only 10 percent (five hundred) would make it through the central file review. As it turned out, there would rarely be five hundred inmates in DTF. Trying to force fit inmates into DTF created big problems: escapes, violence, and so on. In addition, the contractors wanted money to keep the facilities open. Eventually the program collapsed.

There were a number of problems with the OSAP contractors during the time I worked there, including the following:

- One of the aftercare facilities was training parolees to compete in cage-fighting matches in Las Vegas.
- Drug-treatment counselors were bringing drugs into prison and having sex with inmates. Also, one counselor was convicted of beheading an elderly man in the community.
- A warden and the Special Emergency Response Team as well as community police raided an aftercare facility and assaulted a counselor.
- An aftercare provider used a syringe belonging to a parolee who was HIV positive to provide insulin to another parolee when they ran out of new syringes.
- Parolees from a DTF aftercare facility escaped, went to a community park, and slit the throat of a teenager.

In addition to these unbelievable incidents, there were fiscal themed incidents. These included the following examples of how taxpayer money set aside for drug treatment was spent:

- One contractor purchased a portable stage and instruments for a band.
- "Therapeutic" carpeting was purchased.

- One contractor combined funds from several contracts to purchase equipment to build a movie studio. DVDs were made and listed for sale on a website. The CDC was offered a discount to purchase the DVDs. The cost of this project was about a half million dollars.

After the last item above was put together, there were purchase documents forwarded to staff in my area for approval. The project was originally presented as an effort by the contractor to build a library of drug-treatment books and films. The first couple of purchase requests were approved; then a couple of the analysts brought to my attention that the "library" project appeared to be a scam. The contractor was building a movie studio. What made this even more suspicious was the fact that the contractor in question was an avid photographer. The equipment being purchased appeared to be for personal use.

The analysts seemed to think it was futile to try and stop this farce, since the contractors seemed to have free rein with the money they were spending. Jim L'Etoile had moved on to the parole division, where he was having problems dealing with sex offenders. I got together with the acting OSAP chief and told him I was going to gather up all the purchase documents related to the movie studio and disapprove everything. Most of the equipment had been purchased before the documents were reviewed.

Not only did the movie studio project spend $500,000, there were requests for approval to spend another $250,000 for more equipment. By this time Mary Phillip had been hired as the new OSAP chief. Philip was an intelligent, likable person, but out of her element working in OSAP. She was not familiar with prisons, inmates, drug treatment, or the contractors.

Mary Phillip arrived but was not able to deal with me and my refusal to approve the movie-studio paperwork. Merrie Koshell had been placed in OSAP to be a conduit to Director Woodford. I don't know if her function was to watch over Mary Phillip or keep an eye on me; probably both. Phillip had already ordered me to sign the equipment purchase authorization paperwork, but I refused. Next she started ordering subordinate staff to sign the paperwork. I met with Koshell and told her that if the director did not intervene and scrap the movie-studio project, I would go to the state auditor and others. I would blow the whistle again. Koshell remained calm but looked like she was going to scream, but instead indicated she would pass that on. Technically I could have filed another whistle-blower retaliation complaint, since Mary Phillip had suggested I find another job. But I didn't want anything personally, only to have the money returned to the taxpayers.

No action was taken by CDC, so I went to meet with staff at the state auditor's office and later met with Senator Speier's staff. Again my complaint was well documented. I also had a letter sent to Matt Cate, the new recently appointed inspector general. The state auditor took no action, the inspector general took no action, but Senator Speier did. A Senate hearing of the government oversight committee was scheduled for November 14, 2005. I was going to be the star witness.

Once the hearing was scheduled, OSAP staff worked furiously to combat my accusations. They had two of Mary Phillip's minions gather mostly useless information in preparation for the hearing. Senator Speier's staff had warned me that they might not be able to protect me from more CDC wrath. I told them I didn't care; I would testify anyway. I felt pretty confident I stood on firm ground. My previous experience with my whistle-blower complaint gave me a sense of power over my situation. I probably was not as powerful as I felt, but I was going to go for it.

CDC had a difficult time figuring out who was going to testify against me; they fired Mary Phillip just prior to the hearing. The department selected Dean Borg from the legislative office to speak on their behalf. I'm not sure if Senator Speier knew what to make of me. Was I a guy with a sense of right and wrong that transcended concerns of retaliation and just an interest in getting along, or was I a lightning rod for controversy? I testified that there were more problems with OSAP that should be looked at. Again the newspapers and television stations carried stories about the $500,000 prison movie studio funded by taxpayers.

Blowing the whistle once could be a fluke or luck, a one-hit wonder. But doing it twice meant there was no way to tell how many times I would do it. Normal threats did not work. The department could not bully me. I had an audience in the media and the legislature, not to mention the PacoVilla blog that kept stirring up the CDC employees. It was always very special to see how Paco covered my antics. On this occasion they reported "The Borg Failed to Assimilate."

I can only imagine how much shit hit the fan in the governor's office and CDC headquarters. The drug-treatment program that helped put the *R* in the new CDCR for "rehabilitation" was under attack. It would get even better. Senator Speier held another hearing in February 2006 regarding OSAP. Evidently my testimony about the drug-treatment program problems brought more problems to the forefront. Some former OSAP staff had brought some information to Senator Speier's office. Knowing how uncooperative CDC had been in the past, subpoenas were issued this time.

Actually adding the *R* to CDC was a rather foolish move. Instead of bringing rehabilitation to the department, it brought criticism for the lack of improvement in inmate behavior. Why would anyone think you could alter an inmate's behavior established after years of crime by his participation in some rather weak "talk therapy" programs? Drug treatment, anger management, and so on are really just bullshit. There are no magic words that will convince a career criminal to change behavior. No special phrases, no spells, no incantations will make a difference and cure the inmates of their criminal behavior.

Just prior to the start of the hearing, the participants met in Senator Speier's office. I was most impressed by Larry Cupler. Larry and I had worked together earlier in OSAP then he moved to the Office of Audits and Compliance as an auditor. When the department found out he would be testifying, they took him off the audit he was working on and had him working out of an old closet. Larry was being subjected to the kind of harassment I was familiar with. I sat next to him when he testified. He was focused and forthright.

The hearing brought out information about the drug-treatment contractors spending money on cars, fancy office furniture, and year-end spending sprees. Jim L'Etoile testified and appeared comfortable with all of the apparent fiscal overindulgence. Another hearing highlight was the rebuttal by the contractors. David Conn from Mental Health Systems was just starting to offer his explanation for the purchase of several cars when a muffled electrical buzz could be heard. David stated he was having a heart attack. He looked pale and was perspiring. The hearing was paused while medical personnel provided assistance.

The hearing continued after the medical emergency. CDC testified briefly and asked to have the OIG conduct an audit of the OSAP operation. Rod Hickman resigned a couple of weeks later; and Jeannie Woodford, about six weeks after that. Both were a combination of ignorant and arrogant when it came to drug treatment and many other areas. To the rescue came Jim Tilton. He had been summarily dismissed by Teresa Rocha back when I was in the initial stage of my retaliation experience; now he was the newest person in charge of the prison system operation.

By December 2006, Frank Russell and Marisela Montes asked me to take over the Office of Substance Abuse Programs as the acting chief. Things were really looking up for me. The department seemed to be pleased with the work I was doing in OSAP, and it looked like I might be appointed to the job on a permanent basis. This was a Career Executive Assignment (CEA) and would require notification to the governor's office. I wasn't sure how this would work out, since I had been a high-profile whistle-blower on two occasions and was seen as an opponent of the drug-treatment contractors. I was informed that the department had officially submitted my name to the governor's office.

In January 2007 the OIG was preparing to issue a report on the substance abuse treatment programs managed by the department, calling it a "billion-dollar failure." The governor's office was concerned about the press coverage that would follow the release of the report. In February my appointment to the OSAP job was pulled, and Kathy Jett was announced as the new director of the Division of Addiction and Recovery Services. A new position was created, "director"; and a new Division, DARS. I was disappointed.

"Kathy is the right person at the right time to take on this critical responsibility," Governor Schwarzenegger said. "There is no one more experienced in addiction and recovery services and no one more committed to making substance abuse treatment the cornerstone of our rehabilitation efforts in Corrections. Reducing recidivism is central to our prison reform efforts and chronic substance abuse is a major factor in recidivism."

Kathy was a friend of Susan Kennedy, the chief of staff for Governor Schwarzenegger. She claimed to be a former drug addict, most recently working as the director of the Department of Alcohol and Drug Programs. I first met Kathy in February 2007 and spent a great deal of time with her to educate her about the CDCR and the old OSAP. She had a reputation of spending most of her time meandering through the state capitol talking to friends in the legislature. One of the first things Kathy told me was, "I asked to be a director, but I should have asked to be a secretary." She was disappointed that there were so many layers in between her and the person in charge of CDCR.

It was evident that Kathy did not ask for her new job; someone had forced her to move to the CDCR. Were the drug-treatment contractors involved? I don't know. The contractors were ecstatic about Kathy taking over the drug-treatment programs in CDC. They saw dollar signs.

One evening in the spring I received a call from Kathy on my cell phone. "Richard, this is Kathy. I need to ask you a couple of questions about our SAP programs."

"I am in the middle of a softball game, Kathy. Can it wait until tomorrow?"

"Can't wait. I am at the capitol helping develop some new legislation, AB 900."

"Kathy, are you representing the department?"

"That's not important. I need to know if we can add four thousand more drug-treatment beds?"

"We can't keep the nine thousand SAP beds filled that we have now. Why would we want to add four thousand beds?"

"We are going to have to add beds."

"If we have to add beds, then make it two hundred. We could use another staff run program."

"They won't go for that. How about three thousand?"

"No. Kathy, we can't accommodate any more SAP beds."

Kathy hung up but called again a few minutes later. "What do you think about 75 percent participation?"

"Kathy, what does that mean?"

"We should be able to make 75 percent, don't you think Richard?"

"Kathy, 75 percent of what?"

She was getting tired of my questions. "I will get back to you later," she said. After all was said and done, we ended up with something called AB 900 that included, among other things, activation of an additional four thousand SAP beds and the 75 percent "participation" requirement.

One of the problems with the drug-treatment programs was that the majority of the inmates with drug issues did not want to participate in the programs. We ended up forcing inmates to take part in the programs. They figured out ways to get out of the programs. This included getting into disciplinary problems so that the department would remove them from the programs. Another problem was the contract providers. Most of the drug counselors hired by the drug-treatment providers were low-paid people with limited skills and, many times, criminal records.

The next morning Kathy asked me to go get a cup of coffee with her. We walked over to the Starbucks next to the train station across from the federal courthouse on Fifth Street. We sat at one of the little round tables with our coffee and made some small talk, then Kathy pulled a napkin out of her pocket, unfolded it, and placed it on the table. She had drawn an organizational chart in blue pen on a light brown recycled Starbucks napkin. It looked like she had put some thought into this during a prior coffee meeting with someone else. Though Kathy knew little about corrections, she had a good idea how she wanted to position herself.

Kathy said she wanted to bring a person by the name of Mary Fernandez in as chief deputy director of DARS and I would be the deputy director. I asked a few questions about Mary: "Who is she? Where does she come from? What does she know about prisons? What does she know about drug treatment?" Kathy indicated that Mary worked at the State Personnel Board. Other than that, she had no background in prison operations or drug treatment. "Kathy, I don't want to work for someone who doesn't know anything about prisons or drug treatment." She responded, "Well, think about it, and we'll talk about it again next week."

I didn't know Mary Fernandez and had nothing against her, but the job at hand was very complex and would be difficult to figure out. I didn't want to be working in DARS without having the decision-making authority. I knew enough about how Kathy operated to know that I couldn't work with her. She possessed only a rudimentary knowledge of prison drug treatment and thought she knew more than she did. Her political connections would make it very difficult to oppose her, even if she didn't know what she was doing.

Two days later Kathy stopped by my office to see if I had changed my mind about the job she had drawn for me on the napkin. I told Kathy I thought about the offer, but I didn't want to work for someone who didn't know anything about prison operations or drug treatment. Kathy then pulled out a piece of paper with another org chart she had put together: option B. This plan had me working directly for Kathy as her administrative assistant. I looked it over then handed it back to her. "Kathy, I don't want to work for you. I have seen how you operate. I have nothing against you personally, but I don't want to work for you." Kathy looked at me with a pair of watering eyes, dejected. For a moment, the silence was deafening.

She paused a moment, then gained her composure. "Well, I hope it works out for you." We talked a while longer. I told her I would help her with advice and recommendations, and she said she would help me. I was never really sure what she meant by that.

Kathy called me a few days later and invited me to come to a meeting in the large conference room over at 1515 S Street. I asked what it was about, but she said she couldn't tell me. I couldn't figure out why she was being so cryptic, but went to headquarters. When I got there, I noticed a lot of what appeared to be security provided by the CHP. I got to the R Street entrance and saw Bob Gore. He said hello. I took the elevator and went to the third floor.

There were twenty to thirty people there, and I sat at the large table next to someone I knew. There was some buzzing and discussion about what was going on. The room became even more crowded—standing room only. Kathy was in the corner and waved to me. She looked like someone had told her she was about to be named most popular kid at school.

Finally the door popped open and in walked Schwarzenegger, surrounded by Susan Kennedy, Bob Gore, and an assortment of others. Arnold was dressed in a green suit with a white shirt and colored tie. I noticed he had shoes that looked like they were made in Poland. He gave some rah-rah speech about AB 900 and mentioned Kathy. After the speech, he made it around the room shaking hands and saying a few words to everyone. When I shook his hand ,I noticed he was shorter than I thought. He seemed about five foot nine or ten in his Polish-looking shoes. He looked me in the eye and thanked me for my work. He seemed very sincere and personable. There was a box of his cigars at the podium he left for everyone to partake if they wanted to. I picked one up and stuck it in my pocket.

10

Audits

My wife and I went up to Victoria for a few days and stayed at our condo to relax and talk over my job prospects. I knew I didn't want to work for Kathy or Mary. The second day we were in Canada, I got a call from Bud Prunty, the undersecretary. He told me that Secretary Tilton wanted to talk to me about working for him as an assistant secretary. I was startled. I knew Jim and Bud, but didn't know anything about the exempt position process. An assistant secretary position had to go through Governor Schwarzenegger's office, so I didn't feel confident they would approve of a whistle-blower working for them, but I told Bud I would meet with him when I got back in town the following week.

I met with Bud when I got back in town. He told me that Tilton wanted me to be part of the Executive team. I told him Kathy had talked to me about working for her, but I was not comfortable with the idea. Bud indicated that Jim thought the job over the audit office would be a good fit for me. I told Bud that if he and Jim thought I could help them out by working in the audit office, then I would be glad to do that. Jim would prep me for the interview at the governor's office.

My interview at the governor's office was odd. I met the interviewers, Alberto Roldan and Bob Gore. They worked for Susan Kennedy. I knew Bob from back in the 80s, when he worked in the press office at CDC. He used to take pictures for the CDC newsletter. Their questions were rather perfunctory for the most part. Then came the kicker. Bob asked me if I could work with Kathy and help her out. I told him the same thing I told Kathy. I would help her out with advice and recommendations. We talked about the whistle-blower stuff, but it appeared they were more interested in having me support Kathy. Bob made a point of telling me that if the governor's office were ever displeased with me for any reason, they would fire me without notice. I told him that was fine with me, and that I could retire at any time as well, but I agreed to stay until the governor's term was up.

After the interview, Alberto took me on a tour of the area. He showed me Schwarzenegger's office, Maria Shriver's office, and the smoking tent. After we were done there, we walked over to a building on the corner of Fourteenth and I streets. We went down in the basement, and there was Kathy. Alberto delivered me to her. Kathy showed me around the basement and introduced me to Deborah Hysen. Kathy and Deborah were part of the Governor's "strike team." They were charged with implementing AB 900. What a crock. This legislation was pieced together with information Kathy and I discussed in between innings of my softball game. I was not too familiar with the construction part of the plan, but this was evidently the part Deborah had to manage. She seemed very competent and optimistic, but maybe unprepared for the quicksand of prison construction projects.

A lot of people started out with good intensions based on ideas that were not always thought out well. There are so many forces at work with the prison system that it is difficult to see where you are, let alone where you are going or how to get there. Various laws determine most of the structure, but politicians, lawyers, judges, unions, regulations, and criminal minds contribute varying degrees of pushes and pulls that make this complex system difficult to manage. Decisions are always made with varying degrees of incomplete information and uncertain outcomes.

It's a place where I found value in having read various books about quantum physics. Gödel's incompleteness theorem, Heisenberg's uncertainty principle, and complexity and chaos theories all provided guidance. Game theory also weighed in. It is impossible to have a complete list of factors to consider when projecting the impact of various changes in the law, parole supervision, or sentencing changes. Even if you were confident of most of the variables, you couldn't tell what the unintended consequences would be. Not sending parolees to prison for technical violations of parole to reduce the prison population could leave them out long enough to commit a more serious crime and incur a longer prison sentence. In effect, this move to reduce the prison population could actually increase the prison population.

The wild card in the attempt to balance all the competing variables is the criminal mind. Inmates and parolees are not like normal people in the community going along with the program, for the most part. These criminals are usually looking for an angle to avoid doing the right thing and getting away with as much as they can. This is a danger of a different kind. They take property from other people, assault, molest, and kill others. That's why they are in prison. Any time there is a slight miscalculation by a prison or parole employee, there is a chance there will be dire consequences. In fact, even if there aren't miscalculations, there can be problems. Bad people figure out ways to do bad things.

Occasionally I would get a phone call from Kathy saying she was in the governor's office and could see my appointment package on someone's desk. She would tell me, "You should be appointed to your new job any day now." I was never quite sure why she was monitoring my job appointment so closely. Finally I got a call from Alberto Roldan. He wanted to information to put together a little announcement on my appointment to the position of assistant secretary, Office of Audits and Compliance. The announcement was posted on the website on June 12, 2007.

Governor Schwarzenegger Announces Appointments

Richard Krupp, 57, of Granite Bay, has been appointed assistant secretary of audits and compliance for the Department of Corrections and Rehabilitation (CDCR). He has served in

CDCR since 1972 and currently holds the position of deputy director of the division of addiction and recovery services. Previously, Krupp held several positions with the department including staff services manager II at the Research Branch, chief of personnel automation in the Office of Personnel Management and correctional counselor II. He began his career with CDCR as a correctional officer. This position does not require Senate confirmation and the compensation is $96,800. Krupp is a Republican.

Later that day I got a phone call from Andy Furillo, a reporter for the *Sacramento Bee* whom I had talked to before. The paper wanted to conduct an interview and take some pictures for the paper. I asked Andy if I could include Steve Kessler in the interview, since he was my immediate supervisor. I cleared everything with our communications office and the governor's office and set it up for the next day. I was never really sure when I dealt with reporters—what they were going to ask and how they were going to piece together their story. I knew if the story came out wrong, I would get a call from Bob Gore making my new job real short.

I didn't prepare for the interview in any way and just spoke off the cuff. Andy was dressed in khaki pants, a red plaid shirt, and a baseball cap. He was slender and would probably not be noticed in a crowd. He brought a photographer and a woman with him who recorded the interview. I wanted to make sure Steve was part of the interview. He was representing the confidence the department and the governor were placing in me. At this point I wasn't sure if people were thinking I would just kick back and coast through the job for a year then retire or if I would be more dynamic. Andy made me feel comfortable, and I spoke to him like I would a friend stopping by for a cup of coffee. The next day the *Sacramento Bee* ran the story on the front page[9]

I was pleased with the story, and the governor's office indicated I had "hit a home run." For the next few weeks, several headquarters executives stopped to congratulate me; I had a pocketful of handshakes. Now it was time for me to show what I could accomplish.

---

9 Article posted in the appendix.

The wasted years were done. I decided to cancel the publication of an article I had written about women and violence. I had been working on a research paper about female criminals. The paper I wrote was somewhat controversial in that I criticized the governor's plan to place thousands of female inmates in community facilities rather than prisons. An academic journal had accepted the paper for publication. Since I was going to be in charge of the audit office, I decided to concentrate on the new job.[10]

I was sworn in at headquarters flanked by Bud Prunty and Steve Kessler, the two undersecretaries, since Jim Tilton was out of town on that day. I couldn't wear a suit for the ceremony, because my left pinkie finger was still in a cast—a line drive had shattered my finger during a softball game. The surgery required me to have some pins and a soft cast for a few weeks. It made for some jokes about having to twist my arm to get me to take the job.

My office was located in the city of Folsom at the old Aerojet facility. When I arrived at my new office, I spent a few hours with the man I was replacing. Steve Stenoski was retiring after filling the position as a retired annuitant. Fortunately, I knew some of the sixty people working in my new office.

The audit office had a lot of good people working there, but years of executive office abuse and neglect had left the stature of the office in shambles. The audits did not get a lot of attention and didn't carry much weight. Senator Speier had recently pushed some changes through that would strengthen the audit function in California. The legislation had been inspired by some of the retaliation hearings involving Larry Cupler. Larry and I had worked together at OSAP and now in the audit office. He and I testified at a senate hearing before Senator Speier. Now Government Code Section 13887 had strengthened the audit function and built in some whistle-blower-type requirements. Essentially, the law required auditors to blow the whistle if government executives didn't do the right thing. Larry and I were now legit.

I took my new position to heart. It would be my responsibility to look out for the taxpayers. I wanted to treat their money as if it belonged to my mother. Don't spend it foolishly. Be conservative.

---

10 The paper is at the end of this book in the appendix.

Don't waste it and don't misuse it. You should be able to tell people what you are doing with their hard-earned tax dollars without hiding behind an uncertain smile.

For my management team, I had Tim Adams in charge of the Internal Audit Branch, Linda Renzelman over administrative functions, Alberto Caton over prison reviews, George Valencia, juvenile facility reviews, Allen Pugnier Information Systems Security and Raul Romero oversaw inmate education program reviews. Kim Holt managed the external audit connections to the BSA, OIG, and other agencies.

The audit staff members seemed excited to work with me but were still skeptical about the support we would get from executive management. They had been burned before. I could only do things one way: straightforward, with no games. I had been told I was politically insensitive and confrontational in a matter-of-fact way. It sounded odd, but I didn't give it much thought. Two tests came my way shortly after I took over the audit office.

The first time I was tested concerned the audit of the Amity drug-treatment program. This had been the subject of one of my earlier whistle-blowing events and a couple of Senate hearings. Our office conducted an audit as a follow-up to the hearings. As a result of the audit, we determined that Amity would not only relinquish the more than $450,000 of movie equipment, but also another $400,000-plus for various audit findings. Amity was appealing the audit findings, and we were getting pressure from outside to settle the case. The auditors had done an excellent job documenting their findings. When I was asked about settling the case, I said no. I knew the department had used lawyers to battle my case; now they could use the lawyers to fight to protect the interests of the taxpayers.

With the support of the secretary and the undersecretaries, we battled Amity through the administrative processes and the superior court. We prevailed and collected more than $400,000 as well as the movie equipment. There were still more contractor problems to clear up, but we pushed forward and collected more than $4,000,000 during the first eighteen months I worked in the Office of Audits and Compliance. Our auditors were doing good work, and the contractors were cleaning up their practices.

The next test involved a whistle-blower complaint I received about a program in San Diego operated by a contractor involving drug treatment and housing for female inmates and their young children. Not only were there contract irregularities, but also there were deaths and injuries to children being reported. We decided to look at the entire women and children's program. There were facilities in several locations throughout the state. The criminal investigation in San Diego was being handled by local law enforcement, so we started our audit at some of the other facilities to avoid interfering with the investigation.

The women and children's programs were managed by Wendy Still, my old friend from the retaliation I went through a few years back. She had political connections and was close to some of the contractors. The scope of the audit expanded to include all of the operation, not just the San Diego facility. Since I had some history with Wendy, I let the auditors operate without any direction from me. I didn't want to influence the audit.

One day in March 2008 all the executive staff were called to a meeting with Secretary Jim Tilton. Most of us knew what was going on. Jim announced his retirement. It was chalked up to health and family reasons, but I didn't buy that for a minute. This move had Kathy Jett's fingerprints all over it. There had been a constant struggle between Kathy and most of the experienced CDCR executive staff. I wasn't sure whether Jim was stymied by her back-door dealings with the governor's office or was just fed up. As a member of the executive staff, I was in a unique position. I had developed a good relationship with the people who had worked in the department for a number of years and had a cordial relationship with Kathy.

A replacement had not yet been announced, but I did see one of Kathy's scribbled org charts lying around. The structure was odd. There were new positions, like chief of staff. It was obvious to me that this new organization was designed for Kathy to be on top. Then something must have gone wrong, because the new secretary chosen by Governor Schwarzenegger was to be Matt Cate, the inspector general at the time. Cate was about thirty-five years old and worked for the attorney general's office in the past. He had a law degree and was well spoken. Kathy took some time off when the announcement was made. This change of fortune seemed significant to me.

It appeared that someone in the governor's office was getting a little worried about Kathy and her ability to deliver on all the promises she had made. She was not going to be in charge of CDCR.

Matt eventually brought with him Brett Morgan as his chief of staff, Elizabeth Siggins as chief policy advisor, and Lee Seale as deputy chief of staff. The new group was familiar with work in a small agency and little outside attacks from the press or legislature. It would be a difficult adjustment for many in the headquarters office. Since Matt was familiar with my legislative hearing testimonies and current audit functions, it was easier for me to make the transition to the new leaders than most. Many of my colleagues left or were replaced. We ended up with an assortment of new people, none of whom had any prior prison experience. Eventually the Cabinet of about fifteen executives had only one member with any CDCR experience of significance.

The only one left with any prison-sense was Scott Kernan. He became undersecretary of operations. He was the only voice of reason left. Although I had prison experience and was an executive, I was not a member of the cabinet.

The new group took over about the time we wrapped up our audit of the women and children's unit operation. It looked like there would be an investigation into the management of the unit, but then Wendy left to work in the federal receiver's office. She didn't last long there after trying to build yoga rooms for inmates. The federal receiver had convinced the court that inmates were dying at an alarming rate due to poor medical care.

No one ever bothered to actually look at the inmate-death-rate issue to determine facts rather accept the bullshit being presented. In fact, criminals are much safer in prison than in the community. They die at a rate three times higher in the community than in prison. No one seemed to care. Facts were irrelevant.

Audit reports were going directly to the new secretary, Cate. He was directly involved in making executive decisions, as required by the government code. After a while he stopped attending audit meetings. During one meeting we were discussing findings relative to audits of a parolee mentoring program. Lawyers would get paid to provide "mentor" services. As it turns out, the "mentors" were taking parolees to the restaurant Hooters, and having "sleepovers" and other questionable activities.

The department was taking appropriate action: canceling the contract. There was one hiccup. The recent executive order from the governor's required all state agencies to post audit reports on their "Transparency" website. The policy advisor and deputy chief of staff were concerned about the contractor's connection to people in the legislature. Evidently the mentoring program had some connection to Senator Steinberg. Furthermore, Steinberg would be instrumental in the upcoming confirmation hearing involving CDC executive staff. The report was posted as required, but it again appeared I was politically insensitive. I really didn't consider political sensitivities to be relevant.

I had expressed concern about the reporting relationship for the audit office when the new group first arrived. The government code requires that the audit office report directly to the secretary, but I was reporting to Lee Seale, the deputy chief of staff. At first I was told that the secretary, chief of staff, deputy chief of staff, and the policy advisor were like one person. If I reported to one, it was like reporting to the whole group, including the secretary. But as time passed, I got the feeling I was being kept away from the secretary.

Lee Seale was a tall Ichabod Crane–looking lawyer. He liked to swim in Folsom Lake and ride his bike in the morning before work. He said he was an atheist who studied religion in college. One of the first times we met he told me he wanted to provide training for the audit staff regarding the proper use of topic sentences. At first I thought he was joking. But he was serious. I never thought of audit reports as literary works and declined his offer. Lee was a hard worker, but did not know how to manage people.

After a short time he had managed to piss off most of the people in my office. He tended to take over other people's work. For the most part, he didn't add or improve anything but just got in the way. He wanted to insert himself in everybody else's business.

He hindered the audits and stepped on people in another area, Computer Statistics (COMPSTAT).

Just before Jim Tilton left, I was given responsibility for the COMPSTAT unit. This small group of about six people was responsible for the collection of departmental data for management purposes. This was basically a time-consuming manual process that was not working. I wanted to utilize existing automated systems to gather the data like I did when I put together the sick leave and overtime data that got me in trouble with Teresa Rocha. I described my plan to the COMPSTAT staff, and in a few days they all left for other jobs.

I was able to get one person in my office to help initially: Michael Frazier. He understood my data-collection ideas and began to set up some plans for me. I tried to hire someone to manage the COMPSTAT unit, but the reputation the unit had made it very difficult. Finally I found Carol Avansino to join my management team. She was a former correctional officer and worked in automated systems operations as well. When I hired her, we talked about my idea to have data collected from various systems. Carol not only got it, but she had an idea that would make the whole process automated.

Over the next ninety days we hired new COMPSTAT staff, designed the new system, and started the data collection. We used the existing positions and spent $50,000. The new system was more robust than other projects that were planned to accomplish less at a cost of more than $1 million. One of the keys to our success was providing information to the people doing the work in the prisons and parole offices. We weren't asking them to provide information for headquarters; we were using information they had already collected and in turn giving them access to statewide data. A warden at one prison could compare operational data with those at other prisons. Executive reviews would still be conducted, but the prisons would have the ability to see where they had problems and try to fix them before the reviews. Everyone liked the system and the process. Carol and her staff were amazing.

Our bottom-up system became a model for other state prison operations and other state agencies. One day we got a call from a legislative committee staffer regarding an upcoming hearing about performance-measure systems. They wanted us to appear at the hearing and talk about COMPSTAT. Carol and I talked about it and thought a live demonstration would be a good idea. We would appear with Michael Frazier working the demo. It would be great for the department.

Lee Seale decided that he would appear at the hearing instead of Carol and me. He knew very little about COMPSTAT or performance measures. Ignorant and arrogant, he just wanted to take control. Later he said he wanted Carol and I to be there in the audience for moral support. Eventually someone intervened and force-fit Carol and me into the appearance, with Lee as the lead.

Other than the opening comments made by Lee, the COMPSTAT presentation went very well. The COMPSTAT staff members were rather disturbed about the Lee factor. He had taken a position exactly opposite the position I like to take. The people who are actually doing the work should take the accolades, not the managers. I don't think Lee was even aware of how his behavior looked to the staff members who made COMPSTAT work. He didn't think he had done anything wrong.

I began having more and more problems involving Lee getting in the way, interfering and causing problems. On December 30, 2009, my office was finishing up an audit report that we were required to submit to the Department of Finance every other year regarding internal control systems. This effort took several months to complete and required special training and standards. I found out that Mary Fernandez, the undersecretary of administration, had a group of her executives putting together their own report. I couldn't figure out what was going on. All of my attempts to work together or at least determine how to proceed were rebuffed. I finally raised the problem to Lee, but he ordered me to back off and not provide our report to Secretary Cate.

When I first got the e-mail from Lee with the order to back off, I was pissed. I was angry, disappointed, and puzzled all at the same time. At first I went to my computer to calculate my retirement options. I could retire in a couple of weeks and actually get a pay increase. I kept asking myself, why should I continue working? Instead of firing off a caustic response to Lee's order, I decided to think about it, talk to my wife, and then check on my attitude tomorrow. I sent Lee the following message: "I am very disappointed."

That evening Calla and I talked it over. She convinced me that I should fight back. The idea felt comfortable. It fit me well, like a comfortable T-shirt. The next morning I put together a plan and a smoking e-mail to Secretary Cate. I would send it out on Monday morning, refusing to comply with Lee's order. By that afternoon I had everything put together, ready to hit the Send button Monday morning just prior to the cabinet meeting.

I felt like I was back in control of my surroundings. If Secretary Cate did the right thing, my office would be moved out from under Lee and instead be reporting to Cate. If things went sideways, I would bring all my information to the state auditor and the joint legislative audit committee. The press was again an unpredictable wild card. Stand or fall, I could retire with the satisfaction that I had fought a good fight. Looking out for the taxpayers, I would state my piece to anyone who would listen. If a taxpayer knew what was going on, the protections over their hard-earned money being eroded, they would be angry; at least that's what I imagined.

On Monday January 4, 2010, I sent the e-mail to Secretary Cate with copies to others. I waited for some kind of reply. The reply was less than I had hoped for. Cate wanted me to talk to Brett Morgan and Lee before going to him. In my experience this is not a good sign, but I decided to talk to Brett and Lee. First Lee talked to me. He was upset, disturbed that I had gone around him. I explained that I had given him ample time to address the problems, and it was time to move on or up in this case. Brett came in about twenty minutes after Lee and I butted heads. Brett said it looked like I might have disobeyed a direct order from Lee. I told him that it doesn't just look like it; I *did* disobey the order. Brett looked dumbfounded.

Sometimes you need to feel your way around to see where the walls, the obstacles, are. Is it worth the effort? In this case I now knew that Lee and Brett were running interference for Matt. It became obvious to me that Matt Cate was not going to get involved;

he was going to look the other way. I prepared a memo to the head of the legal office, but that was a waste of time. There was no point of continuing to work in the department. For the past year or so I was actually taking home about a thousand dollars per month less than I would if I retired, due to furloughs. I liked working with the people in my office, but Lee was too much of an ass to continue working with. I was disappointed with the lack of leadership from the secretariat.

I retired in June 2010 after thirty-eight years in the CDC. Was I "rehabilitated" as indicated in a news article that ran after my governor's appointment in 2007? Maybe I just continued my behavior in a different setting?

EPILOGUE - Wrap up

Harsant

Maggie Smith, one of the few people at work who would talk to me, used to work for Jim Tilton and was familiar with my current situation. Maggie worked on genealogy as a hobby. She agreed to do some Internet searches to track down Harsant's relatives. Amazingly, it took her only a few days. Once Maggie provided the family tree information to me, I began searching online. Within a few hours, I found phone numbers for people who were related to Harsant. I enlisted the assistance of one of Harsant's friends, Marilyn. She worked at Park Place as an in-home care worker. She was about fifty but looked much older. Years ago she had been involved in drugs and alcohol, and you could see the toll it had taken on her small, slender body. She smoked excessively and swore like a truck driver. Marilyn was always supplementing her income by steam-cleaning carpets or doing some unspecified work on the Internet.

Marilyn and I started making phone calls, and before you knew it we had made contact with nephews of Harsant and finally his son. Turns out Harsant had relatives in Los Angeles; Denver; Battle Creek, Michigan; and Africa who were actually searching for him. I got a call from his son one evening when I was walking through the parking lot after shopping at Home Depot. "Hello, this is Harsant Tantsi. Is this Richard?"

I was stunned. "Yes, this is Richard. Are you Harsant's son?"

"That's me." We talked for about fifteen minutes. I told him I would be visiting Harsant in the morning and would place a phone call so they could talk.

I contacted an investigative reporter I knew, Stephen James. He occasionally wrote stories for the *Sacramento News and Review.* "Stephen, I have a great story for you. A man who hasn't seen his son in forty-seven years is reunited." We talked about Harsant and the upcoming family reunion that would be taking place. A few months had passed since the family contacts started, and Harsant had moved into an assisted-living facility in West Sacramento after suffering through some problems associated with medication. Stephen was invited to join us for the reunion. He could take pictures and interview people, but I insisted that the focus of the story be Harsant and his son. I had been in the papers and on the news quite a bit. I did not want to have Harsant and his son share the spotlight with me; they should have all the attention.

Reunited: Harsant Tantsi meets up with his only son for the first time since the 1950s.

Apologies and Larry

One thing that many people who have been involved in retaliation ask for is an apology from the people responsible for the retaliation. Given the way lawyers taint the process, this is a request that will never be accommodated. However, by happenstance I had an opportunity to make a difference. During the Senate hearing regarding the substance-abuse-treatment contractors, Larry Cupler testified. He had been subjected to retaliation as a result. His complaint took a while to make it through the process, but eventually the paperwork ended up in my hands.

A CDC lawyer met with me to go over the final settlement. I was told that Larry wanted to get back some of the leave credits he used during the retaliation as well as an apology. I was advised that we could probably whittle down the settlement. An apology, of course, was out of the question. Since it was my decision, I signed off on Larry's case for his full request. After doing that I walked over to Larry's office. Larry was working on his computer. Other staff members were close by.

"Larry, how are you?" He looked busy but stopped working to greet me. "I just got the paperwork on your case." He knew what I was talking about. "I signed off on your full request." He looked relieved that it was over. "Also ... I know I wasn't in charge of this office when you were subjected to the retaliation, but I want to apologize on the behalf of the office and the department. What you had to endure was wrong, and I am sorry for everything." Larry looked amazed and grateful. We shook hands, and I went back to my office.

Me and Post-Retirement

After I retired I worked briefly as a retired annuitant for a few days. I was helping the department prepare for some legal battles. However, the chief of staff had me dismissed from my duties. I wasn't actually hired, so technically I wasn't fired. Frankly, I am glad my services were no longer desired. I had no faith in the leadership of the department or the direction coming from the governor's office. Foolish ideas were coming from the governor's office, such as "realignment." One idiotic idea was that prison inmates could be better dealt with at the county level. By the time these people got to prison they had already failed at the county level.

To think that a large number of people end up in prison for non-serious, nonviolent crimes is simply wrong. There is a big difference between a commitment offense and the long list of crimes and victims connected with these criminals. Somehow involuntary manslaughter can be considered non-serious and nonviolent. These attempts to decriminalize crime are misguided ideas from the ignorant and arrogant. The leaders of the prison system should educate legislators and governors about the inmates they manage, not act as meat puppets for them.

The most recent publication from CDC regarding recidivism, the **2011 Adult Institutions Outcome Evaluation Report,** has a section on the drug-treatment programs. Table 24 shows that of the approximately fifteen thousand inmates who participated in the prison drug-treatment programs in CDC who were released, the recidivism rate was about 66 percent. During that same time period, the rate for those who did not participate in drug treatment was about 65 percent. For those released from prison for the first time, the recidivism rate for drug-treatment participants was about 61 percent, versus about 57 percent for those who did not participate. The only logical conclusion that can be drawn from these figures is that in-prison drug-treatment programs are of no value if the objective is to reduce recidivism rates. In fact, the report states, "Given this finding, at first blush it would appear there is little value offered by the in-prison SAP."

However, instead of sticking to the facts, they go on to talk about the small group of inmates who complete the in-prison drug-treatment program and the aftercare program. Though this group represents about 8 percent of the participants, there is no mention of possible selection bias or other variables. This small number of positive outcomes is dwarfed by the 92 percent who not only do not show improved recidivism rates, but also actually show worse recidivism rates. In effect, the CDC and the taxpayers are spending more than $100 million each year for programs that result in higher recidivism rates.

A former drug-addict inmate was hired to replace me as the assistant secretary of audits and compliance. The ignorant and arrogant put a former criminal in charge of security audits, contractor audits, and so on. Within a few months, things began to fall apart and investigations, administrative leave, and so on followed.

I wrote a series of articles for the blog Pacovilla.com. Since I started out with my retaliation experience, I found a great deal of support from the people connected with the blog and from the bloggers themselves. The mainstream media has faded away; some of the investigative reporters I have dealt with in the past are now working for various state agencies.

I still read nonfiction books on occasion, but not as much as when I was working. I am more interested in some of the new music I find on YouTube. A lot of the young people have some interesting observations and good sounds as well. Maybe some people will spend the time and effort to ask enough questions and do enough critical reading, and the will necessary to push the ignorant and arrogant aside.

In order to reduce the prison population to comply with the court-ordered prison population reduction to 137 percent of design capacity, the "realignment" boondoggle was developed. This moves thousands of state prison inmates to county jail facilities. Presto … change-o. The state prison problem is gone. It is now a county problem—then a community problem.

The alignment problems will grow because:

1. The county facilities are not designed for long-term sentences.
2. The medical problems associated with prison inmates will overwhelm the counties.

3. There are not enough activities for jail inmates.
4. The criminals have been sent a message: "Some crime is not that bad."

As a result the following will occur:

1. There will not be enough room in the county jails for all of the misaligned criminals and the prior tenants.
2. It will cost everyone more money.
3. Crime will increase.
4. There will be more problems for law enforcement.

While California is experimenting with realignment designed to make releasing criminals from prison a good idea, the criminals are laughing at us. As reported in the *Sacramento Bee*, Kelvin Peterson and Bernard Krungerrun laughed and smiled after they were sentenced to prison for life without parole after killing a man during a pharmacy robbery. These career criminals were amused by the imposition of the lengthy sentence.

Be skeptical of politicians and government officials. Some of them are like the mythical shape-shifters: They will be different things to different people. They have no real form or substance. The answers they provide are designed only to get you to stop asking questions.

APPENDIX

Articles Posted on Pacovilla.com

A number of problems confronting the CDC surrounded the federal receiver. I addressed this subject in another paper posted on Pacovilla.com:

Deaths in California Prisons

How concerned should the taxpayers be?
June 7, 2010

From 2001 through December 2009, between 343 and 356 inmates died each year while incarcerated in the California Department of Corrections and Rehabilitation (CDCR). How should prison officials, judges, legislators, and, ultimately, California taxpayers view this information? How do these numbers compare to the general population in the community? If the numbers are deemed unacceptable, how much effort and resources should the State redirect to provide remedies?

According to a recent editorial in the *Long Beach Press Telegram*, a federal judge appointed a prison health-care receiver because California state prison inmate healthcare is inadequate and sometimes leads to premature deaths. The receiver plans to "take $8 billion [from the state budget] over the next 25 years." He wants $250 million up-front, right now, to get planning started—that's one-fourth the total cost of the ultra-modern, high-tech new UCLA hospital, just for planning.[11] An additional $3.1 billion would be taken to begin construction.

Local communities have expressed concerns about the recruitment of staff by the prison system to work in medical facilities. It can be a zero-sum game. "We have lost nurses to the prisons in the past, and so there is concern of losing nurses and licensed psychiatric technicians to the prison system."[12] Prisons tend to be located in smaller communities with limited medical resources. Medical staff working in the prisons means fewer to work in community medical facilities. The prison system in California now transports about 1,000 inmates each month into the community for medical treatment. This not only requires Correctional Officers to transport the inmates to the community hospital, but they also are stationed there to guard the inmates during their stay. This means fewer community medical beds accessible to members of the community.

Essentially prison health care is being contracted out to the California Prison Health Care System (CPHCS) and/or community hospitals. It has been reported that 32 states contract out some or all prison health care services. A recent study conducted by the University of California, Santa Barbara examined whether contracting out improved the prison health care system. They found that a "20 percent increase in percentage of medical personnel employed under the contract increases mortality by 2 percent."[13]

---

11 Elias, Thomas (2008). Do prisons need these hospitals? *Press-Telegram*, Long Beach, CA. November 22, 2008.

12 Nisperos, Neil, Hospitals fear worker loss to medical center. DaileyBulletin.com. December 11, 2008.

13 Bedard, Kelly, and French, H. E. *Prison Health Care: Is Contracting Out Healthy?* Presented at the International Health Economics Association convention in Copenhagen, July 9, 2007.

DISCUSSION

Until recently, the available research regarding deaths in prison custody has been limited. The United States Department of Justice (USDOJ), Bureau of Justice Statistics provides statistical reports on medical causes of inmate deaths in state prisons. There is also some research available from sources outside the United States.

An Australian study found that, "custody, notwithstanding its well known dangers and shortcomings, has the effect of reducing or eliminating some of the hazards that confront young adults in the community, and the most important of these are traffic accidents. Also, in prison there is less opportunity for illegal drug use, there are fewer options for suicide, and there is also some level of surveillance and medical care, even if less than perfect. Prison clearly provides some degree of protection...."[14] This study also found that offenders serving community correction orders had a much higher risk of death than the general community and prisoners.

The *New England Journal of Medicine* (NEJM) recently published a retrospective cohort study of more than 30,000 persons who were released from the Washington State Department of Corrections from July 1, 1999, through December 31, 2003. "Overall, the mortality rate among released inmates was 777 deaths from all causes per 100,000 person years (95% CI, 707 to 852). In contrast, the calculated mortality rate for Washington State residents of the same age, sex, and race as the former inmates was 223 deaths per 100,000 person years."[15] The mortality rates for Washington State residents in the NEJM study were derived from the Wide-ranging Online Data for Epidemiological Research (WONDER) system of the Center for Disease Control and Prevention.

The leading cause of death among released inmates was drug overdose, followed by cardiovascular disease, then homicide. The study went on to state, "Our estimates for the study period showed

---

14 Biles, D. (1994). Deaths in custody: The nature and scope of the problem. In A. Liebling and T. Ward (Eds.), *Deaths in Custody: International perspectives* (pp 14–27). London: Whiting and Birch.

15 Binswanger et al. (2007). Release from Prison—A High Risk of Death for Former Inmates. *New England Journal of Medicine, 356*:157–165.

that the risk of death was sharply higher after release than during incarceration, perhaps because there are fewer overdoses, homicides, or motor vehicle accidents during incarceration. In-prison mortality rates reported by the USDOJ Bureau of Justice Statistics for 2001 and 2002 (244 deaths per 100,000 prisoners in state correctional facilities; 192 deaths per 100,000 Washington State prisoners) were also considerably lower than among former inmates."

The USDOJ Bureau of Justice Statistics report on state prison deaths from 2001 through 2006 lists the mortality rate per 100,000 state prisoners by state.[16] The national average was 250 inmate deaths per 100,000 state prisoners. The rate for California during that time period was 213 per 100,000 state prisoners, and reflects that 37 states have higher mortality rates than the CDCR. In addition, there were several states that had substantially higher mortality rates than California, including but not limited to: Pennsylvania (346), New York (257), and Louisiana (402). Some highlights of the report include this following:

- "State prison inmates had a 19% lower death rate than the adult U.S. resident population; among blacks the mortality rate was 57% lower among prisoners."
- "Inmates age 45 or older comprised 14% of the State prisoners from 2001 to 2004, but accounted for 67% of all inmate deaths over the same time period."
- "Two-thirds of illness deaths resulted from pre-existing conditions."
- "The top three causes of death in State prison inmates 2001-2004 were; Heart diseases (27%), Cancer (23%), and Liver diseases (10%). Deaths attributed to Unspecified illnesses or Unknown causes were listed as the cause of death in less than 4% of the State prison inmate deaths."
- "More than 90% of the State prison inmates who died in prison had served more than 24 months at the time of death."

---

16 United States Department of Justice (2008). *Medical Problems of Prisoners, 2004*. Bureau of Justice Statistics.

A recent editorial in the *Mississippi Clarion-Ledger* regarding Mississippi's high inmate mortality rate attributes the deaths to most inmates being "chemically dependent when they land in prison, from drugs or alcohol, with health problems ranging from liver, heart and lung problems, to poor diet and dental disease, and it's no wonder prisons are not models of health, whatever the amenities provided." [17]The article goes on to state that Mississippi routinely ranks at or near the top in obesity, diabetes, high blood pressure, and cardiovascular problems among its general population.

In the 2004 Survey of Inmates in State and Federal Correctional Facilities,[18] a report on medical problems of prisoners was published. The survey reveals that approximately 44% of the state inmates reported a current medical problem, with 70% of those reporting seeing a medical professional because of the problem. Almost all (96%) of the state inmates reported they were tested for tuberculosis. Among state and federal inmates surveyed, current medical problems were most commonly reported by those who were homeless in the year prior to arrest (51%), used a needle to inject drugs (60%), or reported receiving government assistance (61%).

For California as well as other states, the number and rate of deaths per 100,000 inmates held in custody varies from year to year. Approximately one-third of the CDCR inmate deaths actually occur in community hospitals where they are sent on temporary release status for medical care. Utilizing WONDER data similar to the NEJM study described previously, the California State resident mortality rate for 2006 for those people 15–64 years old was approximately 256 per 100,000 population. This rate is slightly higher than the CDCR inmate death rate (242) for the same year. Parolee deaths are not included in this analysis. For 2002 and 2003, there was an average of approximately 118,000 CDCR inmates on

---

17 *Mississippi Clarion-Ledger.* Inmates: Death sentence? Or free health care? November 25, 2008.

18 United States Department of Justice (2008). *Medical Problems of Prisoners, 2004.* Bureau of Justice Statistics.

parole.[19] During that time, 819 parolees died in 2001, 859 in 2002, 869 in 2003, and 849 in the following year.

CDCR Inmate Deaths

2001–2009

Year	CDCR Inmate Deaths[1]	Average Daily Prison Population[2]	CDCR Rate/100,000[3]	National Rate/100,000[3]
2001	290	157,142	178	242
2002	327	159,695	213	246
2003	315	161,785	207	258
2004	332	163,939	213	253
2005	352	168,035	223	254
2006*	397(428)	172,528	242(249)	250
2007*	368(397)	171,444	215(230)	
2008*	345(369)	171,264	201(216)	
2009*	364(396)	169,958	214(233)	
1. CDC R Data Analysis Unit				
2. CDCR Data Analysis Unit				
3. USDOJ				

* Data from 2006–2009 from CPHCS in ( )

Note: During the course of this study, it became evident that there are some data quality issues. The number of inmate deaths reported by CDCR and by CPHCS (in parentheses) is not consistent. For example, in the table above the number of inmate deaths for 2006–2009 indicates different reported totals. An audit should be conducted to determine the actual number of inmate deaths each year. The different numbers also produce different inmate mortality rates.

---

19 California Department of Corrections. (2004). *Parole Population Movements.* Offender Information Services Branch.

DISCUSSION

One of the difficulties with the examination of in-prison inmate death data is identification of the comparison group. In-custody populations vary substantially from the community at large, "the validity of comparing the prison population with the general population has been questioned, as these groups differ in terms of age, sex, ethnicity, social class, alcohol and drug misuse and physical and mental health."[20]

Inmate mortality rates must be examined in context of differences between deaths in prison and deaths in the community. The population demographics are substantially different and need to be adjusted if the rate comparisons are to be meaningful. Not only are there vast differences from state to state in general population demographics, but there can be large differences between general population within a state and the prison population within the same state. Mortality rates can differ to a significant degree by ethnicity, age, and gender.

---

20 Sattar, G. (2001). Rates and causes of death among prisoners and offenders under community supervision. *Home Office Research Study No. 231*. London: Home Office.

CALIFORNIA POPULATION DEMOGRAPHIC DATA

	California State Population	CDCR Population*	WONDER Crude Mortality Rate
Gender			
Male	49.5%	93.4%	318.6
Female	50.5%	6.5%	190.0
Ethnicity			
Black (Male)	6.5%	29.1%	597.6
Hispanic (Male)	32.6%	39.8%	229.6
White (Male)	46.5%	25.1%	385.7
Other (Male)	14.4%	6.1%	177.5
Black (Female)	7.4%	29.0%	342.3
Hispanic (Female)	30.5%	30.1%	119.1
White (Female)	46.4%	35.9%	240.1
Other (Female)	15.7%	4.9%	107.3
Age			
<1–14	21.3%	0	516.6
15–19	7.5%	1.2%	
20–24	11.0%	12.3%	85.1
25–34	14.4%	32.2%	84.4
35–44	15.1%	27.2%	154.4
45–54	13.8%	20.0%	378.5
55–64	9.5%	7.2%	790.6
65–74	5.5%	**	1794.0

*2009 data   ** CDCR data for 55–64 includes 65–74 age group

With adjustments to the California demographic data, a comparison can be made between the prison mortality rates and the community rates utilizing data available through WONDER and CDCR/CPHCS. Previously all mortality data reported by state prisons to the USDOJ and various state reports combined all racial categories and both genders. The most glaring discrepancy is seen in the gender proportions. In California there is an approximate even gender breakdown in the community, but in the prison system almost 95% of the population is male. Significant differences in some ethnic and age categories can be seen as well. Given that WONDER data shows significant mortality rate difference along these same parameters, adjustments are required to adequately compare prison to community mortality rates.

Utilizing WONDER[21] data from 2001–2006 and information from CDCR population reports,[22] adjusted mortality rates can be developed to provide a similar community comparison rate.

California Population Male and Female Mortality Rates

15–64 years old, all races

	WONDER Crude Rate	WONDER Age Adjusted Rate	CDCR Ethnicity Adjusted Rate	CDCR Ethnicity Adjusted Age Rate
California Female Rate	190.0	212.2	237.1	236.0
California Male Rate	318.5	368.0	372.8	406.2

---

21 Centers for Disease Control and Prevention, National Center for Health Statistics. Compressed Mortality File 1999-2006. CDC WONDER Online Database, compiled from Compressed Mortality File 1999–2006 Series 20 No. 2L, 2009.

22 California Department of Corrections. (2004). *Parole Population Movements.* Offender Information Services Branch.

Combined Male and Female Rate	255.0	293.9	309.8	**363.7**

How does the adjusted population compare with other data?

	Mortality Rate
California Adjusted WONDER Rate	**363.7**
CDCR 2001–2006 Average	212.7
CPHCS 2006–2008 Average	231.5

Utilizing the California Adjusted WONDER Rate of 362.7, the number of expected deaths in CDCR for 2008 would have been 664. The actual number of deaths reported by CPHCS was 345 with a 215.5 rate.

In 2007, there was a significant increase in medical staffing and related costs in the California prison system. The CPHCS "hired 172 new primary care physicians between August 1, 2007 and July 31, 2008".[23] In addition, CPHCS "added 488 registered nurses and 533 licensed vocational nurses to the health care delivery system." However, no noticeable difference in the number deaths either in prison or in the community on temporary release is evident. In 2006, there were 252 in prison and 145 temporary release community hospital deaths. In 2007 there were 222 and 146, respectively; and in 2008, 194 and 151.

California "will spend $2.2 billion this year to treat, house, and guard physically and mentally ill inmates, a 550 percent increase since 1995. The prison's population grew about 30 percent during that same period. Annual health care spending has increased

---

23 Imai, Kent. (2009). Analysis of Year 2008 Death Reviews, December 14, 2009, California Prison Receivership.

from $2,714 per inmate in 1995 to $13,778 this year, according to the State Department of Finance." [24]

In the recent CPHCS report, Analysis of Year 2007 Death Reviews, it is noted, "In 2007 there were 397 California inmate deaths.... The vast majority of the deaths, 83 percent (327 cases) were identified as non-preventable." [25] The 2008 report indicates there were 82 percent (303) non-preventable deaths. The report lists 16 percent as possibly preventable. This is lower than the 23 percent noted in the article regarding a Veteran's Administration study cited on page seven of the CPHSC report (discussed in greater detail in next section).

For 2006 the CPHCS report reflects 66 "Preventable/Possibly Preventable" deaths for 2006, 68 for 2007, and 66 in 2008. The number of "Non-preventable" was 358 in 2006, 327 in 2007, and 303 in 2008, with "Suicide/Homicide" accounting for 59 in 2006, 55 in 2007, and 45 in 2008. "The death review process was less standardized in 2006." [26] No conclusions can be drawn from this data.

NUMBER OF DEATHS BY PREVENTABILITY—CPHCS DATA

Year	Likely Preventable/ Possibly Preventable	Non-Preventable	Suicide/ Homicide
2006	18 / 48 (total 66)	358	43 / 16 (total 59)
2007	3 / 65 (total 68)	327	33 / 22 (total 55)
2008	5 / 61 (total 66)	303	38 / 7 (total 45)

24 Thompson, Don, (2008). Federal judges to rule on Calif. prison crowding. Associated Press, December 1, 2008.

25 Imai, Kent, M.D. (2009). Analysis of Year 2008 Death Reviews, December 14, 2009, California Prison Receivership, p. 8.

26 Imai, Kent, M.D. (2009). Analysis of Year 2008 Death Reviews, December 14, 2009, California Prison Receivership, p. 18.

The CPHCS report concludes that, "death rates in the CDCR are significantly decreasing in part because the high-quality CPHCS peer review process has resulted in the replacement of 85 potentially dangerous providers with new well-qualified providers."[27] Neither the data nor the analysis provided in the CPHCS report supports this conclusion. The report does not indicate how many of the 85 providers were hired by the CPHCS.

In the latest report on 2008 death reviews, CPHCS indicates 85% of the CDCR inmates deaths were judged to be "non preventable." Of the remaining 66 deaths, 61 were "possibly preventable," and 5 were "likely preventable." The determination of preventability is more of an art than a science. A *Journal of the American Medical Association* study found the inter-rater reliability among reviewers was low with agreement about one-third of the time. Given these loose parameters, it does not appear there should be any precise conclusions drawn.

DEATHS DUE TO MEDICAL ERROR

According to the *Journal of the American Medical Association* (JAMA) study mentioned in the CPHCS report, "Similar to previous studies, almost a quarter (22.7%) of active-care patient deaths were rated as at least possibly preventable by optimal care, with 6.0% rated as probably or definitely preventable."[28] If the level of medical care in CDCR is similar to care in the community, it would be within prevailing rates to expect approximately 77 or 23% of the 340 deaths from the above-referenced table. This would be equivalent to about one inmate death every six days in CDCR.

Though the CPHCS report makes "no attempt to estimate the impact of preventability in terms of life expectancy"[29], the JAMA study went on to determine how long the patients would have lived if not for medical error. It found that "many deaths reportedly due to medical errors occur at the end of life or in critically ill patients in

---

27 Imai, Kent, M.D. (2009). Analysis of Year 2008 Death Reviews, December 14, 2009, California Prison Receivership, p. 26.

28 Hayward, Rodney A., Hofer, Timothy. (2001). Estimating Hospital Deaths Due to Medical Errors. *The Journal of the American Medical Association, 286:*415.

29 Imai, Kent, M.D. (2009). Analysis of Year 2008 Death Reviews, December 14, 2009, California Prison Receivership p. 7.

whom death was the most likely outcome, either during that hospital-ization on in the coming months, regardless of the care received."[30]

CONCLUSIONS

The adjusted overall in-custody death rates for CDCR are lower than national prison rates and California community rates. There has also been evidence to support the position that the population we are looking at may be less at risk for some causes of death while in prison than in the community. Nationwide de facto inmate mortality rates have been established as reported by the USDOJ.

Given that the USDOJ reports that most deaths in prison are attributed to heart disease, cancer, and liver diseases, it is unlikely that improving the quality of medical care would lower the mor-tality rate for inmates. When comparing the established de facto in-prison mortality rates with community rates, it appears that inmates are safer in prison.

By their very presence, in-prison custody staff members ensure relatively quick medical services are available to state prisoners. However, in the community, it is unlikely that similar services are available to this group. Any influx of funding intended to improve the level of care available to inmates would most likely not improve inmate mortality rates.

In prison, there is less opportunity for illegal drug use, fewer options for suicide, and some level of surveillance and medical care, even if less than perfect. Prison clearly provides a greater degree of protection. It is noted that almost three times as many people die each year while on parole than in prison. It appears that individuals incarcerated in the correctional system are less likely to die while under the supervision of in-prison correctional staff than when they are in the community under less scrutiny and left to their own devices.

It is difficult to justify spending taxpayer dollars to improve what appears to be an expected rate of inmate deaths in prison

---

30 Hayward, Rodney A., Hofer, Timothy. (2001). Estimating Hospital Deaths Due to Medical Errors. *The Journal of the American Medical Association, 286*:418.

when there are certainly higher priorities for health care or other improvements in the community. "It simply makes no sense to mandate building the equivalent of eight new UCLA Medical Centers strictly for use by society's most destructive elements."[31] It is sometimes overlooked that most of the inmates we incarcerate are locked up precisely because they have victimized people that certainly are more deserving of any tax dollars that we may consider spending on lowering the in-prison death rate. "It is ironic that those who are supposed to be punished for crimes can get paid health care that law-abiding folk cannot afford."[32]

All CDCR inmates in effect have complete medical insurance coverage at no cost to them, but a high cost to the taxpayers. There is no evidence that the high prison medical expenditures contribute anything to reduce inmate mortality rates. In fact, given that the mortality rate for California inmates is already substantially lower than a similar demographic group in the community, it makes no sense to continue to spend large sums of taxpayer dollars for this endeavor.

Projections and Uncertainty

Is It a Quantum Physics Problem?

November 28, 2011

In a recent *Los Angeles Times* article some counties are complaining that the "Re-alignment/Misalignment" procedure has sent more inmates their way than had been projected." For instance:

- Los Angeles County was projected to add about 600 state prisoners by now but has booked more than 900.
- Orange County's transfers are running more than double what the state estimated.

31 Elias, Thomas (2008). Do prisons need these hospitals? *Press-Telegram*, Long Beach, CA. November 22, 2008.
32 *Mississippi Clarion-Ledger.* Inmates: Death sentence? Or free health care? November 25, 2008.

- Riverside County is now at 93% capacity and will be full by January.

Has there been an error in the projections? A brief look at the projection process may be helpful. The Department of Corrections has been using a complex inmate population projection system for a number of years to help determine how many inmates they need to house in the upcoming years.

The Bureau of State Audits (BSA) reviewed the prison population projection system in 2005 and found, "the projection is useful for assessing the next two years' budget needs but has limited usefulness for longer-range planning, such as the need to build new prisons." For example, BSA found, "the department's fall 1995 projection forecast that the inmate population would exceed 232,000 in 2001. However, the actual population in 2001 was 161,000, a difference of 71,000 inmates."

If we look at the spring inmate population projections going back to 2006, we can see what the 2011 inmate population was projected to be, compared to the actual population on November 14, 2011, of 155,258. As with most projections, the farther out you look, the less accurate you will be. As in quantum physics, in any measurement there is an element of uncertainty. In this case, it is not a shortcoming of the projection calculation, just a product of the large number of variables and various adjustments made by outside processes.

Projected 2011 inmate population

Year of Projection	Projected Population	Difference from actual	Error Rate
2006	193,195	37,937	20%
2007	186,148	30,890	17%
2008	167,535	12,277	7%
2009	172,205	16,947	10%
2010	164,671	9,413	6%
2011	161,546	6,288	4%

The closer you get to 2011, the smaller the error rate. Outside variables that can impact the projections include the following:

- **Adjustments**—Los Angeles District Attorney Steve Cooley said his office is teaching its lawyers to "scour" criminal records to make sure they note any prior offenses when they file new charges, and to make sure that new charges include offenses categorized as serious, violent, or sexual when possible.
- **Proportionality**—With more than 150,000 beds/cells the Department of Corrections can much more easily handle a few hundred inmates than a county with a few hundred or a few thousand beds/cells.
- **Bed Days**—The Department of Corrections typically makes room for inmates that stay in prison for more than an average of two years. County jails typically house inmates for closer to two months. At this rate one prison inmate is equivalent to six jail inmates as far as bed days are concerned.

Recent viewpoints expressed by Roger Warren of the National Center for State Courts and Barry Krisberg of UC Berkley have been supportive of the "misalignment procedure." In part the hope is that "evidence-based treatment programs" will cure the inmates of their criminality if they stay at the local level. Unfortunately there is little if any "evidence" that any program will "cure the inmates" of their criminal behavior. This is actually a major outside variable. Criminals are not likely to view the "misalignment procedure" as a procedure they want to undergo.

Criminals may view all of these misguided "procedures" as an opportunity to take advantage of the criminal justice system. For example, the murder rate in Stockton went up 50% in 2010 compared to the prior year and with the 54th murder a few days ago* is set to surpass last years' total. California citizens are likely to bear the brunt of the misalignment one way or the other.

*The 54th murder broke the Stockton record.

Some Ways to Reduce Government Waste and Inefficiencies

Cruel to be kind

March 11, 2011

Governor Brown asked the Bureau of State Audits and the Little Hoover Commission last month for ways to reduce government waste and inefficiency. I worked in the California prison system almost 40 years. About a third of my time was spent in the prisons working as a Correctional Officer and Counselor and the last two thirds in Headquarters, managing the inmate drug treatment programs, then internal audits, eventually retiring as an Executive appointee in 2010. As the administration and the legislature struggle with the budget and taxes it appears that corrections will play a lead role in the setting of priorities. Having studied corrections research and working in the system, I have some observations and recommendations to offer.

Much time and money is spent on inmate problems that are overstated, irresolvable, or nonexistent. The last administration "settled" some inmate lawsuits that were founded in legal alchemy by lawyers who have made a great deal of money at taxpayers' expense. The new administration should concentrate on undoing this "public harm." How did this happen? The book _Legal Alchemy, The Use and Misuse of Science in the Law_ by David Faigman provides some insight. Here are some highlights:

- Most lawyers have little or no appreciation for scientific method and lack the ability to judge whether proffered research is good science, bad science, or science at all.
- Many lawyers seem to suffer from "syndromic lawyer syndrome," a pathological acceptance of simplistic explanations for complex human behavior that supports otherwise desirable legal outcomes. Peddling policy as science permits opponents to corrupt the "science" to their own political objectives.

- Because they are not held accountable for their knowledge, legislators feel little pressure to truly deal with the complexities of science. Only the conclusion counts. The reasoning or principles that underlie the conclusion are of minor legislative concern.
- The more strongly the political outcome is desired, the more likely the science, however certain it might be, will be manipulated, ignored, or rebutted.

In an effort to cut the cost of incarcerating criminals in state prison, funding for inmate drug treatment programs should be eliminated and excessive inmate medical care spending should be drastically reduced.

1. Much of money spent on inmate medical care by the Federal Receiver is unnecessary and has no impact on inmate health, mortality rates, or suicide rates. In fact the medical care inmates receive exceeds community standards. Much of the money is spent on bloated salaries and headquarters management. In many cases there is duplication of the staffing in the prison and/or CDCR headquarters operations. Data presented to support the billions of dollars wasted on this effort is typically slanted, overstated, and intellectually dishonest. Available legitimate data indicates inmates are safer and healthier in prison than they were before they were committed and quickly go back to unsafe, unhealthy patterns when they are released. The proposed Fiscal Year 2011–12 budget is about $1.75 Billion. No amount of money will alter this pattern.

2. Drug treatment programs in prison do not work. By the time people have earned their way to prison, they have already been through drug treatment programs in the community, been on probation, been sentenced to time in county jail, and been threatened with prison. Many of them were in prison before. The two things that have the biggest impact of future drug use are old age and death. Drug treatment programs for inmates and parolees typically find that

criminals find their way back to prison faster than those not participating. Talk therapy has no magic words that will cure the inmates of their drug abuse. The programs are generally run by private contractors. Many instances of criminal behavior and waste of taxpayer money have been found with little evidence of positive outcomes. The proposed fiscal year budget is about $140 million.

3. Corrections would be best served concentrating on the reduction of the "sensitive needs yard (SNY)" inmate status that drives up operational problems and associated costs. With a SNY designation the prison removes the inmate that is being pressured and wants to behave and work, labeling him a "snitch." Instead, the predatory inmate should be placed in a general population "non-programming yard." A lock-up unit requires complex due process be provided to the inmate. In a non-programming "Spartan" general population unit with less privileges, the inmate holds the key to his return to a programming unit by participating in the classification process and agreeing to comply with the Department's rules on inmate behavior and accepting a work or training assignment.

Sometimes you need to be blunt and say things that appear to be cruel in order to move forward and make tough decisions. The taxpayers need to feel confident their money is being spent wisely.

Put Focus on Women for State Prison Reform?

If wishes were horses, then beggars would ride.

April 9, 2011

On April 9, 2011 the *Sacramento Bee* ran a "Special to the *Bee* Viewpoint" from Judy Patrick, CEO and president of the Women's Foundation of California. Evidently Ms. Patrick had recently visited the two women's prisons in Chowchilla and had an opportunity to meet and talk with them. She was "heartened by their resilience and determination." About half of the women can now be released to community supervision, according to Ms. Patrick, because they are nonviolent, low-level offenders with children they need to raise.

Ms. Patrick and the *Sacramento Bee* may want to take a look at a paper I wrote in 2005 regarding this issue, "Women Offenders and Violent Crime, Victims of Trauma? Monstrous, Crazy, Evil, or Dangerous. Paradoxes and Conundrums." Here are some highlights:

Are women offenders, the victims of trauma and abuse or are they increasingly becoming more violent both in the community and in prison? Are these two scenarios mutually exclusive? Trauma and other life problems are commonly associated with explanations for female criminality. According to Stephanie Covington, "The female offender's life is shaped by her socioeconomic status; her experience with trauma and substance abuse; and her relationships with partners, children, and family. Most women offenders are disadvantaged economically and this reality is compounded by their trauma and substance abuse histories."

Various theories concerning women's "pathways to crime" include elements of; trauma, post traumatic stress disorder, surviving abuse, low vocational and education skills, etc. In most of these areas comparisons to reported rates for men are described. Though some of the differences may be attributable to self-report variations, there may still be substantial differences between men and women on some of these elements.

Some light can be shed on this subject by looking at the victim selection of women who commit violent offenses. There are many current cases that can put faces on the numbers and may provide clues toward understanding the dynamics involved. Typically women offenders victimize other women, the elderly, or children. One of the most vulnerable victims is a pregnant woman. As described by Professor Sherry Colb (2005), Rutgers Law School, "a pregnant woman is in a condition that distinguishes her from all other people—men and women alike—who are not pregnant. She holds a second life within her body."

Lisa Montgomery befriended Bobbie Stinnet through the Internet (CNN.com, Freed & Flores, 2004). She pretended to have an interest in the puppies Stinnet was raising and selling. On December 16, 2004, after being invited into Stinnet's home, Montgomery strangled the eight-month pregnant woman to death, cut open her abdomen, and stole her baby. Shortly after the murder and kidnap, Montgomery was showing off the baby as hers at a restaurant.

Peggy Jo Conner of Pennsylvania was arrested on October 15, 2005, for a vicious attempted homicide. Conner hit her eight-month pregnant neighbor over the head with a baseball bat, then proceeded to cut the victim's abdomen in an attempt to take her unborn child. Fortunately a teenage boy stumbled upon the crime scene and notified his father, who called the police. Both the mother and child survived the attack. Conner's attorney plans to hire a psychiatrist to determine why a law-abiding caring person would commit such a heinous act. Are there any mental health-related explanations for this behavior?

The connection between Conner and the victim was characterized as "a close friendship." When the police arrived on the scene, Conner offered to move her car to make room for the ambulance. In her car, police found evidence of pre-meditation: a knife, syringe, gloves, and a hemostat [surgery clamp].

Gender Responsive Theories and Strategies

In Stephanie Covington's paper "The Relational Model of Women's Psychological Development," she states that "five patterns of relational disconnection may foster substance abuse and increased risks of relapse in women: (1) non-mutual relationships, (2) effects of isolation and shaming, (3) limiting relational images, (4) abuse, violation, and systemic violence, and (5) distortion of sexuality." Covington goes on to describe how the feelings of isolation and shaming "may come to feel increasingly monstrous, crazy, evil, or dangerous."

In describing Jean Baker Miller's book *Toward a New Psychology of Women*, Covington states, "She suggested that for women the primary motivation throughout life is toward establishing a basic sense of connection to others." The Bureau of Justice Statistics (BJS) estimates that 62% of the violent female offenders had a prior relationship with their victims, while only 36% of male violent offenders were estimated to have known their victims. It might be more accurate to say that all human interaction involves the establishment of connections and relationships. This cannot be characterized as an attribute found only in women.

In the previously described incidents where women attacked pregnant women to "harvest" a child, relationships had been established. The victims knew their assailants and posed no threat. Since 1987 there have been 10 documented cases of "Newborn kidnapping by Caesarian section." Half of these cases occurred since 2000. In a study looking at 199 cases of abductor violence in non-family infant kidnapping, abductors were usually women who had a prior relationship with the victim-mother. The authors stated, "When comparing infant kidnapping with other violent crimes, the number of times when this type of crime results in the death of the victim is extremely high, and the number of violent crimes committed by women is increasing."

Current Arrest and Incarceration Trends

According to a report from the Urban Institute regarding a similar time period, "While the rate of female incarceration has risen, there has not been a corresponding rise in violent crime among female offenders. In fact, the proportion of women imprisoned for violent crimes continues to decrease as the proportion of women incarcerated for drug offenses increases (Covington, 2002, p. 68)."

Trends, of course, may appear different depending on the time period you are looking at. If we look at the 2000–2004 time period, we find the previously described trends (1989–1998) have reversed. The BJS reports, "For every category of major crime for the period 1990–1996—violent, property, drugs, and other felonies—the rate of increase in the number of convicted female defendants has outpaced the changes in the number of convicted male defendants (BJS, 2004)." The report goes on to state, "Since 1995 the annual rate of growth in the number of female inmates has averaged 5%, higher than the 3.3% average increase of male inmates (BJS, 2004)."

The Federal Bureau of Investigation Uniform Crime report indicates for "Current (2004) Year Over Previous Year (2003) Arrest Trends," total offenses charged for males up 0.4%, but for females the increase was 2.9% (BJSI, 2004, P289). Also, for murder and non-negligent manslaughter, males were up 2.7% and females up 13.2%. The figures are even more alarming for the under-18 age group. Male arrests were up 19.4% and female arrests were up 38.6% for murder and non-negligent manslaughter.

For the most part, women offenders target other women as their victims. In a special report on women offenders published in 2000, the BJS states that, "three out of four victims of violent female offenders were women (BJS). Children and the elderly are also commonly victims of female criminals. "Women commit the majority of child homicides in the United States, a greater share of physical child abuse, an equal rate of sibling violence and assaults on the elderly, about a quarter of child sexual abuse, an overwhelming share of the killings of newborns, and a fair preponderance of spousal assaults."

According to the BJS, "Between 1976 and 1997 parents and stepparents murdered nearly 11,000 children. Mothers and stepmothers committed about half of these child murders (BJS)." In Canada, between 1974 and 2000, 460 fathers and stepfathers were accused of killing their kids and 400 mothers and stepmothers.

The elderly are also often victims of violent women offenders. On October 13, 2002, a 47-year-old California woman initially denied knowing anything about the killing of her 70-year-old husband. His body was covered with cuts, 27 wounds, and 15 stab wounds, half a dozen of which penetrated his flesh. Next she claimed self-defense, but couldn't explain why she didn't call the police and left the body for her 15-year-old son to find the next day. The arresting authorities indicated the woman told them, "Oh well, we were getting a divorce anyway."

Judy Gellert had been employed as a substance abuse treatment counselor at the Richard J. Donovan Correctional Facility in San Diego. She testified against her crime partner, 42-year-old Marcia Johnson. The two sold a house and car belonging to their victim, a 71-year-old man, months after they reported him missing to police. Johnson told the detective, "I was so mad at him, I cut his head off with the chainsaw. And then I cut both of his feet off. But when I cut his head off, I didn't realize how heavy a head is." The body parts were then wrapped in Saran Wrap and aluminum foil before placing them in a Rubbermaid container and burying them.

Gellert and Johnson had established an ongoing close relationship with the elderly victim in this case. Was there any indication of past trauma in the lives of the two women involved in this murder? Gellert went to college, had stable employment, but did have a drug abuse history. Johnson had drug and mental health problems. In addition, she told a reporter that she would describe stories of her past molestation by a neighbor and mistreatment by her mother, to "make people feel sorry for me and get what I want."

Current California State Prison Trends

Women in prison are also becoming more violent. Inmate Toledo at California's Valley State Prison for Women, died on October 16, 2005, as a result of an altercation with another inmate on the yard. About 60 days later, on December 20, 2005, two women got into a fight at the same prison. Inmate Duran beat and strangled her cell partner, Yglesias, to death, according to a report in the *Los Angeles Times*.... In 2003, of the 33 state prisons in California, staff members at one of the women's prisons were assaulted on 67 occasions; 48 of the assaults involved weapons. The rate of assaults per custody staff at that institution is one of the top ten for assaults on staff in California.

For women, the proportion in California state prisons for crimes against persons in the year 2000 was 25% (2617), but by 2004 it was up to 30% (3148). The proportion in prison for murder/manslaughter went from 9.6% (1060) to 11.7% (1230). For "Assault with a Deadly Weapon/Assault and Battery" violations, there was an increase from 7.5% (816) to 10% (1041). (Updated figures for 2009 are included in the table below.)

Trends 2000–2009

Women in California State Prisons

Proportion by Year

Crime Category	2000	2004	2009
Against Persons	25%	30%	35%
Drugs	42%	29%	24%
Property	28%	36%	35%
Other	5%	5%	6%

* 2000, N=10,427   2004, N=10,671 2009, N=10,812
** Data source CDCR (2010)

The California Department of Corrections is now embarking on a plan to move a large number of female inmates from a traditional state prison setting to a series of smaller community-based facilities. This movement is in part based on the gender-responsive theories and strategies. The smaller facilities would provide "gender-based" services that would include substance abuse treatment, anger management, trauma management, vocational and educational training, etc.

There is a general lack of evidence to support the theory that gender-based programs produce different outcomes than traditional models. "The literature on gender differences in treatment needs points to gender-specific needs but conclusions are often not empirically based. The outcome literature, still very sparse, has not yet incorporated the literature on gender differences in pre-treatment characteristics and has not yet provided information on what components of gender-specific treatment are necessary to produce more successful outcomes for the female substance-abusing population."

In the "Female Offender Gender-Responsive Housing Plan" (2005), it states, "women are less likely to be convicted of violent offenses, pose less danger to the community and are more successful in community-based therapeutic programs." The current arrest and incarceration trends run contrary to California's plan. The Leo Chesney Center, a private-contracted female community correctional facility, under contract with the Department of Corrections was evaluated in 2002. Concerning return-to-prison rates at six months, one and two years post-release, the evaluation indicated that there was no difference in the return-to-prison rates between the women at the Leo Chesney Center and the comparison group of women housed in California's state-run institutions (CDC, 2002).

The "Gender-Responsive Housing Plan" proposes that a large number of low-level and nonviolent women be moved to community-based facilities. The number of inmates falling into this category is estimated to be about 4,000. However, this estimate does not take into account criminal history, various medical issues, and other criteria that may preclude placement in community-based facilities. It is likely that the actual number of women meeting the criteria for placement in these facilities will be substantially less than the estimate of 4,000.

The Canadian Experience

Following a 1990 task force report on women in corrections in Canada, the Canadian Prison for Women was closed and the women offenders were moved from this central location to smaller regional facilities. One of the weaknesses of the task force report was that it did not address the small portion of inmates at the maximum-security level who could not function in a community-type living unit. This was a new approach and both its strengths and weaknesses became apparent fairly quickly, as detailed below.

In 1996, in one of the institutions, there were a number of serious incidents including suicide attempts, serious assaults on staff, seven escapes, and a homicide. There was no perimeter fence at the time. Following "unrelenting media attention," the higher-level custody women were transferred out of the regional facilities. The maximum-security inmates were later moved to separate and distinct units in the men's prisons until solutions could be developed (the co-located units all closed between 2003 and 2004). The minimum- and medium-security women remained in the regional institutions. Additional static security (perimeter detection fence with razor wire, cameras, etc.) was added.

These Canadian incidents were described in the book, *When She Was Bad*, by Patricia Pearson. "A new facility in Edmonton, Alberta, for all the Prairie Region's female inmates, responding to arguments made by Canada's Elizabeth Frye Society that women are only in prison because of men's abuse, and that if you treat them with respect, they'll conduct themselves with dignity. As indicated above, no security fence was erected around the perimeter, and no locks were put on the 'bedroom' doors. Within the first six months, 7 of the inmates escaped. One inmate was apparently hanged in her room by others who simply let themselves in." The inmates that escaped were apprehended quickly; some phoned and asked to come back.

Between March 1999 and April 2002 there were twelve hostage-taking incidents. Nine of the incidents occurred in one of the women's units in the men's institution, one occurred in one of the new institutions, one in a psychiatric center, and one at a provincial institution that also accommodated federal women. The majority of the inmates involved in these incidents were not committed to prison for violent offenses.

In an exploratory investigation, the Correctional Service of Canada (CSC) determined that less than one-third of the commitment offenses were assault-related for the female perpetrators involved in the hostage-taking incidents. However, about two-thirds of the women had a history of assault-related offenses. Half of the inmates had been assessed as doing well in their programs prior to the hostage-taking incidents.

Staff were taken as hostage in six of the incidents. In ten of the incidents, the inmates used weapons. During one hostage incident, inmates tortured a female correctional officer. The hostage-takers were asked to comment on the impact of their actions on the correctional officers. Words in their description included "traumatized," "physically scarred," "mentally damaged," and "long-term damage." One inmate questioned the impact, stating, "they exaggerate … they portray themselves as the victim, as whiney."

A report commissioned by the Union of Canadian Correctional Officers (CSN) indicated that the CSC had "underestimated the level of risk represented by female offenders, when judging them to be far less violent than men." The report also found that contrary to the expectations of the CSC, the opening of new, smaller facilities for women was actually accompanied by an increase in violence.

The report went on to indicate that the CSC treated women "as if they could be characterized by only moderate degrees of risk, security and needs, as if it would suffice to confine them in a normalized environment and provide them with more or less elaborate treatment and training programs, in order to rehabilitate them." The normalization of inmates via rehabilitation has been characterized by the union as a failure.

On November 3, 2005, a maximum-security inmate at the Edmonton Institution for Women scaled two internal fences, but not the perimeter fence, and nearly escaped. The *Edmonton Sun* reported, "The circumstances that bring women into conflict are different than those of men. For that reason women have different needs." According to the president of the UCCO, "We cannot understand why there are two levels of security for inmates for male and female institutions. Society is protected differently according to gender. If you're a criminal, you're a criminal." Women have the same security levels as men, based on the same criteria, institutional adjustment, risk of escape, and risk to the public. Static security measures may be used differently in men's versus women's institutions.

Where Do We Go from Here?

Violent women offenders present paradoxes. "We cannot insist on the strength and competence of women in all the traditional masculine arenas yet continue to exonerate ourselves from the consequences of power by arguing that, where the course of it runs more darkly, we are powerless. This has become an awkward paradox in feminist argument." How can we explain a woman attacking a pregnant woman to take her baby? Are both the victim and assailant victims of trauma? If both are victims, is anyone responsible for the horrific crime? What about the babies?

If women have such an array of handicaps working against them when they enter the criminal justice system, including trauma, lack of educational and vocational skills, etc., why do they generally have lower return-to-prison rates than men? Fiorentine et al. have described this conundrum as the "gender paradox."

When designing gender-responsive strategies for the custody and supervision of women offenders, the criminal justice system must remain cognizant of the growing trend toward violence. Women have demonstrated escalating violent behavior both in the community and within correctional facilities. The state of Minnesota is spending millions of dollars to erect double fences around their state prison for women due to the increase in the number of dangerous female offenders.

According to Steve Salerno in his book *SHAM*, "Victimization has eroded time-honored notions of personal responsibility to a probably irrecoverable degree." He goes on to state, "Victimization, which sells the idea that you are not responsible for what you do (at least not the bad things)." Criminal offenders must be held responsible for their own behavior and subsequent rehabilitation. Without this personal accountability, "Even murderers sometimes cease to become murderers and instead become victims of the conditions that made them murder."

The victims targeted by female offenders are primarily other women. Children and the elderly also are often victims of women. The primary concern of the criminal justice system should be for the victims of criminals, not the perpetrators. The safety and security of the community and the correctional facilities that house criminals should outweigh unproven rehabilitative programs. "Once you make allowances based on people's weaknesses, where do you draw the line? And who gets to draw it?"

Should all women who commit crimes be viewed as victims and not as offenders? A Canadian report, *The Transformation of Federal Corrections for Women: Myths and Realities*, argues that, "It is true that many women offenders come from socially disadvantaged backgrounds and that their lives have been characterized by poverty, violence, and physical and/or sexual abuse. However, women offenders do commit serious crimes that harm others and compromise public safety."

If all women offenders are perceived as victims of abuse, trauma, economic disadvantages, etc., and not fully responsible for their own criminal behavior, we do a great disservice to the real victims. The real victims are the women, children, and elderly that female offenders assault and murder at a rapidly expanding rate. As one corrections official stated, "If a female offender is holding a knife to your throat, you don't really care weather or not she was molested as a 12-year old because you can't deal with history and causes during a crisis." Incarceration with appropriate classification and custody considerations should be primary; the testing of rehabilitative theories should be secondary.

From blowing whistle to calling the shots

By Andy Furillo—*Bee* Capitol Bureau

Published 12:00 am PDT Friday, June 15, 2007
Story appeared in MAIN NEWS section, Page A1

Print | E-Mail | Comments (16)| Digg it | del.icio.us

Richard Krupp, once demoted after refusing to fudge figures, says he'll be able to help solve problems in his new role. *Sacramento Bee/*Anne Chadwick Williams

When Richard Krupp refused to fudge the numbers on sick leave and overtime costs, he found himself shuffled off by management into a nothing job in a nothing corner of the state prison system.

Now, he's going from being banished to being the boss. Earlier this week, the Schwarzenegger administration appointed Krupp, the most prominent prison system whistle-blower this decade, to lead the effort to root out waste, fraud, and abuse in the correctional agency.

"They pulled me out of the hole I was in and kind of gave me a new lease on life," said Krupp, 57, who will take over Monday as the head of audits and compliance for the California Department of Corrections and Rehabilitation.

It's a promotion that represents even more vindication for the 35-year civil servant. Krupp was awarded $500,000 in October 2004 when the state agreed to settle his whistle-blower retaliation lawsuit and other legal claims.

More than the money, the new job puts him in position to do what he really wants: fix things that go wrong.

"Now, I can actually help solve some of the problems," Krupp said in an interview Wednesday. "This is an opportunity to help rather than just point the finger."

Krupp comes into his $96,800-a-year job—no Senate confirmation is required—with accolades from his new boss and from the legislative staffer who helped bring him back from the bureaucratic dead. He even got a tip of the cap from the former corrections director Krupp blamed for some of his past trouble.

"What better person to head audits and compliance than someone who has spent a lot of time raising issues that needed to get fixed and didn't get anywhere," said corrections Undersecretary Stephen Kessler, to whom Krupp will report.

"Now, Richard can raise those issues, and part of his job will be not only raising issues, but identifying options and solutions to make things better," Kessler added. "Doing the right thing shouldn't be really hard."

A career correctional employee who started out as a line officer in Chino, Krupp eventually worked his way to the headquarters division in Sacramento in 1985. Within a decade, he had been promoted to chief of the personnel automation section.

In 1999, Krupp found himself in the middle of a conflict between his correctional bosses and the California state auditor who derailed his career.

The auditor's office had finished a study that found the corrections department blowing $29 million a year on sick leave and overtime. Corrections managers assigned Krupp to write the department's response. He concluded the problem was worse than the auditor had reported.

"When I raised those issues, I was told to make the report look like we were actually improving the situation," Krupp said, identifying a retired warden as the official who gave him those instructions. "I told him I wouldn't do that."

Next thing Krupp knew, he was taken off the response project, removed from his job as the personnel automation boss, and reassigned to the research bureau with a new title: staff services manager II. His new job: reviewing student requests to interview inmates.

Cal Terhune was the corrections director at the time Krupp was moved into his obscure post. In an interview this week, Terhune said he was "annoyed" by the auditors' conclusions because they compared the prison system's sick leave to the Highway Patrol's. It was "a bum comparison," Terhune said, because it was easier for a patrol officer to see a doctor while on shift.

Terhune denied that the department retaliated against Krupp. "I was trying to get the guy promoted," he said.

Terhune said Krupp struck him as being "analytical" and "research-oriented" and termed Krupp's promotion a good move.

"That's where he should be," Terhune said. "His talents are in research and program evaluation, and he is an idea person. He's very strong in that area."

Krupp said he knew "things would happen" as a result of his whistle-blowing. Now, he's an expert on the subject and what it takes to be one.

"You have to learn to suffer well," he said.

While in the research bureau, Krupp, who holds a doctorate in criminal justice from Claremont Graduate University, read up on complex systems theory, economics, and quantum physics. He also came across some transcripts from prison oversight committee hearings in early 2004. He wrote a letter to committee co chair Jackie Speier, the former Democratic senator from Hillsborough, who asked Krupp to testify.

"He's the biggest whistle I've ever run into in my 28 years in government," said Richard Steffen, the Speier staffer who coordinated

Krupp's committee appearance. "He got pressured, but he didn't go under."

More whistle-blowing followed. Working since 2002 in the prison system's inmate drug-treatment division, Krupp found out that a private in-prison drug-treatment provider, the Amity Foundation, was using state-purchased videotaping equipment to film its staff training programs. Whether that was appropriate became the subject of another Speier hearing in 2005, and the foundation is still being audited, according to Amity chief Rod Mullen.

"I hope he can help, in terms of CDCR's compliance issues," said Mullen, who otherwise declined to comment about Krupp.

When he starts his new job Monday, Krupp said, he plans to review in-prison drug treatment as one of his first orders of business. Then he said he intends to bring back "peer review" audits in which teams of correctional professionals travel from prison to prison to see what works and what doesn't.

Business services, automated systems, food services, procurement, and, of course, sick leave and overtime, also will draw his focus, Krupp said.

"I'm hoping I can help the administration do some things the right way and make some good decisions, save the taxpayers some money, and make the community safer," Krupp said. "That's our main objective."

www.ingramcontent.com/pod-product-compliance
Lightning Source LLC
Chambersburg PA
CBHW070014300526
45794CB00001B/314